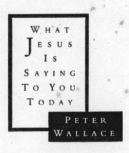

WHAT JESUS IS SAYING TO YOU TODAY

PETER WALLACE

WHAT JESUS IS SAYING TO YOU TODAY

PETER WALLACE

OLIVER NELSON

THOMAS NELSON PUBLISHERS
Nashville • Atlanta • London • Vancouver

Published in Nashville, Tennessee, by Thomas Nelson, Inc.,
Publishers, and distributed in Canada by Word Communications, Ltd., Richmond, British Columbia.

Unless otherwise noted, Scripture quotations are from the
Contemporary English Version. Copyright © 1991, American
Bible Society.

Scripture quotations noted NKJV are from THE NEW KING
JAMES VERSION. Copyright © 1979, 1980, 1982, Thomas
Nelson, Inc., Publishers.

Library of Congress Cataloging-in-Publication Data

Wallace, Peter M.
    What Jesus is saying to you today / Peter Wallace.
       p.   cm.
    Includes index.
    ISBN 0-8407-9202-6 (pbk.)
    1. Jesus Christ—Words—Prayer-books and devotions.
2. Devotional calendars.   I. Title.
BT306.W35   1994
242'.2—dc20   94-16043
                                     CIP
Printed in the United States of America.

1 2 3 4 5 6 — 99 98 97 96 95 94

For my wife, Bonnie,
daughter, Meredith,
and son, Matthew

INTRODUCTION

My goal is that you not think of this thing you hold in your hands as a book nor even as a daily devotional. I hope you will think of it instead as a doorway into the presence of your heavenly Father, who welcomes you and delights in your spending time with Him. Or think of it as a springboard, launching your mind and catapulting your heart into personal meditation and communion with the Lord.

What Jesus Is Saying to You Today is the first in a series of daily reading collections designed to be flexible and interactive. The format enables you to follow along as you feel most comfortable, and it encourages you to be open to the Spirit's leading in order to find the truth you need at the moment you read it.

There are at least three ways you can read this book.

1. *You can read it a page at a time, a day at a time.* Each page is marked with the number of the day. You can start out with Day 1 on January 1 and finish up with Day 366 on December 31 (there's an extra reading included for leap years). Of course, this is the traditional way of reading devotional

books. And you may find it most convenient for you. But consider a couple of alternative ways.

2. *Pray first, asking the Lord to direct your reading.* Then flip the book open to a page and read it. Or scan the verses to find one that hits you where you are. You may find you need to read two pages or even three at one sitting to find the one that speaks loudest to you in your need at the moment.

3. A Subject Index is located in the back of the book to help you find a reading that focuses on a particular concept. So if you're feeling lonely or spiritually hungry, or if you want some insight on following Jesus or reaching out, *look up these words and select a reading* that focuses on them. In this way your daily reading focuses on something relevant in your life at the moment.

You may think of yet another way to use the book. I hope you do because my goal is to encourage you to hear Jesus' words as though for the first time. To hear them as though they were spoken directly to you. And to respond to them personally.

To this end, I encourage you to begin your time every day in prayer, to ask God to open your heart and mind to His insight and His will. Then read the page you've selected. Record your thoughts and prayers in a journal. Let the reading launch your meditation on Jesus' words, focusing on how they can be reflected in your life today. Then follow with a time of prayer, asking God to help you respond in whatever way He wills.

This isn't a devotional book; it's a workbook. The comments I've included are designed to prod your heart and mind. I hope you will use this book to help you think and work through your struggles and frustrations in life. Let it be a guide to peace and serenity with your God.

If you benefit from using *What Jesus Is Saying to You Today,* consider reading future volumes as well—*What the Psalmist Is Saying to You Today* and *What God Is Saying to You Today.*

I would like to express my heartfelt appreciation to the special people in my life today who have contributed to my thinking and who challenge me to walk the path toward spiritual health and wholeness. They include my wife, Bonnie, my pastor, Gray Temple, Jr., Dr. Fred Hall, Harold McRae, and my close friends Cary McNeal, Ken King, Jon Franz, Alan Charters, Dean Picha, David Hodge, Wesley Greer, Jonathan Golden, and many others. All are precious to me beyond words.

May God open your eyes through the reading of Jesus' words. And may my comments not get in His way or yours.

—Peter Wallace
Stone Mountain, Georgia

Jesus left Galilee and went to the Jordan River to be baptized by John. But John kept objecting and said, "I ought to be baptized by you. Why have you come to me?" Jesus answered, "For now this is how it should be, because we must do all that God wants us to do." Then John agreed.

—Matthew 3:13–15

The first recorded words of Jesus in the Gospels are a request to be baptized by John—despite John's impassioned protests. Yet Jesus persisted because, to put it simply, it was the right thing to do.

Sometimes you may think the things God requests of you—an encouraging word to a stranger, an act of sacrifice, a gift of your time or money—make little sense. But when you know it's the right thing to do, take the risk. Follow John's example of humble obedience. Then watch what happens.

In John's case, a voice from heaven resounded, and a dove descended.

Wonder what will happen in your case?

The Scriptures say: "No one can live only on food. People need every word that God has spoken."

—Matthew 4:4

Jesus was hungry—desperately hungry. At the Spirit's leading, He had survived for forty days without food in the desolate wilderness in preparation for His ministry.

Then the devil showed up and encouraged Jesus to take the easy way to satisfy His hunger.

Jesus had every right to turn rocks into rolls. But He had made the decision to rely completely on His Father, to draw strength and nourishment from His Word, and to trust Him.

You may feel you're languishing in a desert today. And you may feel alone, hungry—spiritually, emotionally, or even physically—and very tempted. See the Father with you there. Hear Him speak to you. What is He saying?

DAY 3

The Scriptures also say, "Don't try to test the Lord
your God!"

—Matthew 4:7

If Satan had been in charge, Jesus' debut could
have been a rather awesome spectacle: jumping
off the pinnacle of the temple, to be whisked
away by angels. It probably would have shocked
a lot of people into becoming His followers.

But that wasn't God's way—not that He doesn't
shock some people from time to time.

Jesus recognized God had a different plan.
And it makes absolutely no sense to try to get
Him to do something that isn't in His will. That's
what Jesus means by "testing" God.

When you examine your requests of Him—
and the motives behind your requests—His
word to you today may hurt a little bit.

Instead of figuring out the answers to your
personal dilemmas, give them to Him. Then listen to His leading. It may not be very spectacular, but it will be right.

Jesus answered, "Go away Satan! The Scriptures say: 'Worship the Lord your God and serve only him.'"
—*Matthew 4:10*

In the wilderness, Satan offers Jesus all the kingdoms of the world if He will fall down and worship the lord of darkness.

But Jesus has had enough. Unshaken, He orders the fallen angel away and clearly reveals where His allegiance lies. Jesus knows the truth. There isn't even a moment of hesitation.

Can you say the same today? How often have you wondered if only I had more money . . . if only I were in a different career track where there was some hope of success . . . if only . . . ?

Jesus was offered the world, and He didn't even have to think twice about it. He knew what held more value by far.

You'll never be offered the world. But you will have to deal with other temptations—even today. Take a few moments right now to prepare yourself to respond.

Then Jesus started preaching, "Turn back to God!
The kingdom of heaven will soon be here."
—Matthew 4:17

Jesus' message to the people of His day was simple and unmistakable: Turn back to God. Turn around. Change your ways. Refocus your life. Move away from your sinful, selfish ways. And move toward God.

Jesus is offering you an invitation. It's an invitation to new life. A life filled with joy and fulfillment. A life that lasts forever in the kingdom of heaven.

That glorious kingdom will soon be here. Tomorrow, it may be a physical reality. But for today, it's here. It's now. It's within you.

Visit there awhile.

Jesus said to them, "Come with me! I will teach you how to bring in people instead of fish."

—*Matthew 4:19*

They were fishermen. Hard workers. Tough. Weatherworn. Strong. Independent.

A stranger approached them, inviting them to come with Him and pursue the souls of men and women.

And they "dropped their nets and went with him" (Matt. 4:20).

What was it about Jesus that caused those tough guys to lay their entire livelihood aside to be with Him?

Was He wearing a nametag that said, "Hello, I'm the Messiah"? No. But they knew He was nonetheless.

Or was it the invitation He gave, which in just a few words offered them fulfillment, purpose, and companionship?

Now ask yourself, What's Jesus inviting me to do today?

God blesses those people who depend only on him.
They belong to the kingdom of heaven!

—Matthew 5:3

Gently, compassionately, Jesus utters words of encouragement on the side of a mountain.

You are there, part of the multitude. You hear Him promise God's blessing on those who depend on Him. And the words ring true.

You know that within you dwells no ability to please God. Your desire is to depend wholeheartedly on God, not on your own resources. You yearn for an overflow of God's Spirit instead of relying on your own spirit.

If that's your goal, if that's your lifestyle, Jesus offers you the kingdom of heaven. It's not something you earn. It's a gift of God.

You may feel spiritually weak. If so, rejoice. It's the perfect opportunity to experience the riches of God's Spirit today and enter into the kingdom of heaven.

God blesses those people who grieve. They will find comfort!

—*Matthew 5:4*

Grieving.

Letting yourself experience sorrow over your circumstances, mourning the loss of something valued, perhaps even lamenting your sin—and its consequences.

Perhaps that's where you are today.

Jesus' word is inviting: Recognize your needs. Then give them over to Him.

He doesn't say the sad feelings will disappear, replaced by joy and freedom. He does say, "They will find comfort!"

In the midst of the despair come winds of hope, an embrace of understanding, the light of a new morning. For joy will indeed come in the morning.

In the meantime, rest in God's comfort.

God blesses those people who are humble. The earth will belong to them!

—Matthew 5:5

Many of us have etched on our brains an image of Jesus as meek and mild. Quiet and shy.

But reading the New Testament should dispel any vestige of that notion. Jesus didn't hesitate to confront boldly, even angrily. He even had the reputation of being a reveler—a partyer.

We know Jesus never sinned. And that fact may prompt us to ask some questions about our behavior today.

When He praises people who are humble, what does He mean?

People who understand their position in relation to the world and to God. People who seek not their own success but God's.

In short, people who don't strive to own the earth.

But guess what they are promised?

DAY 10

God blesses those people who want to obey him more than to eat or drink. They will be given what they want!

—Matthew 5:6

Let's face it. Some days we just aren't very hungry for obedience to God. We get too comfortable in our own desires, our own opinions, our own conveniences, our own pleasures.

Maybe today is a day like that for you. Try as you might, you just can't make yourself be thirsty for God's will.

If so, admit it. Don't force it. Let it go, just for today.

But before you do, ask God as sincerely as you can to increase your appetite for Him. Day by day. Moment by moment.

That's a prayer He'll delight in answering, perhaps sooner than you think.

And you'll delight in His answer, too.

God blesses those people who are merciful. They will be treated with mercy!

—Matthew 5:7

The car in front of you cuts you off. The store clerk gives you a hard time with your return. A client tells you one of your competitors has been spreading some false accusations about your business. A child breaks a treasured knickknack.

Life is full of opportunities for you to be merciful. To treat an offender compassionately. To be forgiving and kind.

Today, Jesus encourages you to be merciful. That doesn't mean to force a rigid smile, to mutter under your breath so no one can hear, or to choke down the anger that rises up.

There's nothing wrong with feeling these feelings—as long as you give them over to your loving Savior when you do.

Let them melt away in the light of His mercy for you.

God blesses those people whose hearts are pure. They will see him!

—Matthew 5:8

In this world, it's harder than ever to live a pure life.

At least that's the excuse we comfort ourselves with. After all, nobody's really pure.

So how can we experience this word from Jesus today?

The first thing is to adopt a realistic attitude toward purity of heart. Understand that it refers to a single-minded pursuit of God, not perfection in behavior or attitude.

Single-mindedness doesn't mean you won't stumble from time to time. But if your goals are right, Jesus says you'll ultimately reach them.

And you will see God.

Take a moment today to examine your heart, your goals, and your desires. Then talk these things over with the God who yearns to be pursued by you.

DAY 13

**God blesses those people who make peace. They will
be called his children!**

—Matthew 5:9

In this day of codependency, peacemaking is
getting a bad reputation.

But Jesus isn't talking about trying to fix people's problems in order to avoid conflict or gloss
over serious problems.

If anyone was a peacemaker, it was Jesus Himself. And if He avoided anything, it certainly
wasn't conflict.

Genuine peacemaking is the spiritual aroma a
true believer exudes. The light in one's eyes that
communicates compassion and acceptance.

It's grace in action, mercy with skin on.

And it comes only by spending time with the
Source of all grace and mercy.

How will you know when you've experienced
it for yourself? Listen to what people call you.

God blesses those people who are treated badly for doing right. They belong to the kingdom of heaven.

—Matthew 5:10

Persecution for one's faith is something we read about but rarely experience personally.

Is that because we live in a Christian nation? Hardly.

Is that because there's a great deal of tolerance of religious expression these days? Think again.

There is one more explanation. But it's one we really don't want to acknowledge because it means we aren't trying to do right.

Jesus isn't asking us to be obnoxious—far from it. He isn't asking us to be perfect; that's His job.

He is asking us to live in obedience to Him as a matter of course and let the chips fall where they may.

DAY 15

God will bless you when people insult you, mistreat you, and tell all kinds of evil lies about you because of me. Be happy and excited! You will have a great reward in heaven. People did these same things to the prophets who lived long ago.

—Matthew 5:11–12

The last thing anybody wants is to be persecuted.

But today, Jesus says people who are insulted and bad-mouthed and picked on and even injured for His sake are specially blessed. In fact, He says it's reason to be excited because, in the end, it will matter.

Today's a good day to ask yourself how blessed you are—by your friends, your family, your work, your recreation, and so much more.

But are you being blessed by God for the hardships you're enduring . . . the risks you're taking . . . the sacrifices you're making . . . the inconveniences you're suffering . . . for His sake?

Take some time today to make Matthew 5:3–12 a prayer for yourself.

You are like salt for everyone on earth. But if salt no longer tastes like salt, how can it make food salty? All it is good for is to be thrown out and walked on.
—*Matthew 5:13*

Jesus' followers naturally season their world around them. And in so doing, they create a thirst in others for their Master.

At least that's how it's supposed to be. Somehow, it doesn't seem to be working that way in our culture.

And Jesus says salt that isn't salty is simply colorless, tasteless, useless crystal. It's irritating grit and good for nothing.

Is it any wonder why we're not making much of an impact in our world—or even our neighborhoods?

Ask God to season you today, to make you tangy and flavorful for Him.

Then get ready to reach out to a lot of thirsty people in His name.

DAY 17

You are like light for the whole world. A city built on top of a hill cannot be hidden, and no one would light a lamp and put it under a clay pot. A lamp is placed on a lamp stand, where it can give light to everyone in the house. Make your light shine, so that others will see the good that you do and will praise your Father in heaven.

—Matthew 5:14–16

Too often, we start the day a little dim, dull, and dreary. There's hardly enough warmth within us to keep the chill off our fingers. The thought of warmly embracing others seems far beyond our capability.

Sit comfortably and close your eyes. See the darkness. Then imagine opening your eyes and seeing a brilliant morning in a fresh, dewy meadow.

Jesus is waiting there for you. His arms are extended to you, ready to embrace. He gathers you up to Himself. The morning sunlight is warm on your face, but the warmth of His compassion and love for you fills your heart. And soon you begin to shine.

Stay there as long as you need to today. Then go about your business. But don't keep that light to yourself.

Don't suppose that I came to do away with the Law and the Prophets. I did not come to do away with them, but to give them their full meaning. Heaven and earth may disappear. But I promise you that not even a period or comma will ever disappear from the Law. Everything written in it must happen.

—Matthew 5:17–18

Jesus' way was revolutionary. His words shocked and even infuriated many people. So much so that the leaders of His own religion had to get rid of Him.

However, He had no intention of destroying the old ways and instituting a different way. He came, ironically, to fulfill what God had already established.

And the reaction of the leaders shows how far humans had wandered away from the way of life God has always called them to live. God doesn't change. But we do—sometimes for the better, sometimes not.

As human beings, we are prone to wander from His ways. Yet relentlessly, He calls us, pursues us, woos us. And when we can hear Him and respond, we can rejoice with Him.

If you reject even the least important command in the Law and teach others to do the same, you will be the least important person in the kingdom of heaven. But if you obey and teach others its commands, you will have an important place in the kingdom.

—*Matthew 5:19*

When Jesus speaks, it's not just an opinion, something we can hear, consider, and accept or reject as the mood strikes us. Jesus' words carry weight. They have the force of the God of the universe behind them.

Sometimes we become so familiar with them that they lose their power for us. We've heard them already. We know them. Perhaps we've even memorized them.

Ask God to enable you to see His Word without preconceived notions. Without the dullness familiarity can cause. Without the frustrated resignation that builds up when we must wrestle with what He's saying because we really don't like hearing it.

Ask God for new eyes to see His Word and a new voice to share it with others.

You must obey God's commands better than the Pharisees and the teachers of the Law obey them. If you don't, I promise you that you will never get into the kingdom of heaven.

—Matthew 5:20

The Pharisees were righteous, God-fearing, respected, and worthy leaders. In their own eyes, that is.

They were intimately acquainted with every penstroke of the law of God. They had it all figured out, and they zealously ensured that the people knew it.

Then Jesus came upon the scene and stunned the people with the pronouncement that unless they were even more obedient to God's commands than the guiding lights of perfect living, they didn't have a chance of getting into heaven.

But upon reflection Jesus' point sinks in. Entering the kingdom comes as a result not of external legalism that is hypocritical to the core but of obedience or righteousness of heart. And that kind of righteousness can result only when God empowers the heart.

Today, examine your heart in the light of God's power.

You know that our ancestors were told, "Do not murder" and "A murderer must be brought to trial." But I promise you that if you are angry with someone, you will have to stand trial.

—*Matthew 5:21–22*

Anger kills. It not only corrupts a relationship, but it can harm the object of anger. And it can eat at the soul of the one who is angry. In fact, Jesus says anger toward someone is just as serious a matter as murder.

Let that shocking comparison hit you.

In a day when we are encouraged to express our anger in order to maintain honesty and keep from bottling up our feelings, these words can sound confusing.

But Jesus isn't saying to deny your feelings. He's saying to deal with them positively. If you feel anger, figure out why. Then go to the person, either for forgiveness or for compassionate confrontation.

Work it out. Pray it through. Deal with it. Before it becomes something deadly.

So if you are about to place your gift on the altar and remember that someone is angry with you, leave your gift there in front of the altar. Make peace with that person, then come back and offer your gift to God.

—Matthew 5:23–24

First things first.

Jesus says if there's a problem between you and someone else, there's a problem between you and Him. So don't try to put it out of your mind or cover it up with a righteous act such as bringing a gift to God.

Make peace with the person. Restore the relationship. Make it right. And in so doing, make it right with your Savior.

Obviously, your relationships with others are important to God. So today would be a good day to think about the significant people in your life, to pray for them and thank God for them, to ask yourself if you're out of sync with any of them, and to express to them personally what they mean to you.

You know the commandment which says, "Be faithful in marriage." But I tell you that if you look at another woman and want her, you are already unfaithful in your thoughts.

—Matthew 5:27–28

It seems Jesus expects a lot of us.

But His word today only proves how dangerous it is to play with the fire of lust.

In today's world, such statements seem archaic. Our culture has become so accepting of loose morals and casual relationships that a strong word against even *thinking* of doing something immoral is truly unsettling.

Think about your attitudes, your habits, your desires. Consider the input you feed your brain—from television, magazines, movies, and even conversations. Then let Jesus' words burn in your heart.

It's serious business. And now may be the time to devote some serious time wrestling with it in prayer.

DAY 24

If your right eye causes you to sin, poke it out and throw it away. It is better to lose one part of your body, than for your whole body to end up in hell.
—*Matthew 5:29*

Sin should never be taken lightly.

Point-blank, Jesus shoots down the notion that sin can be frivolously dismissed as just part of being human.

Yes, it *is* part of being human to sin. But it shouldn't be frivolously dismissed.

Sin is serious business because it can devastate your relationship with God, with those you sin against, with other believers in the body, and even with yourself.

We can be thankful that God overflows with forgiving grace. And He is willing and able to give you the strength you need to stand strong against any temptation.

Today, take Him up on His offer to protect you from stumbling.

Keep holding His hand.

When you make a promise, say only "Yes" or "No." Anything else comes from the devil.

—Matthew 5:37

If you have to swear by God, Jesus says, that proves you don't always tell the truth.

His followers, by contrast, should develop the reputation of being utterly forthright. So when you say something, there's no doubt that you mean it. When you say yes, others can rely on the fact that you'll follow through. And when you say no, there's no need to try to cajole you into reconsidering.

Jesus' words are always trustworthy. There's never any room for doubt and uncertainty.

His followers should speak no less boldly.

Is He willing to help you do so?

Yes.

You know that you have been taught, "An eye for an eye and a tooth for a tooth." But I tell you not to try to get even with a person who has done something to you. When someone slaps your right cheek, turn and let that person slap your other cheek.

—Matthew 5:38–39

Some people accuse Jesus of expecting us to be doormats, to let others treat us in whatever ways they want—even if it hurts.

But doormat Christians are weak. And it takes a great amount of strength to stand up to someone and turn the other cheek. In fact, that takes more strength than most humans are able to muster.

Jesus is telling us to avoid the spirit of revenge. Vengeance is God's job, not ours. And if we feel we've been slighted in some way—or even physically injured—we need to turn it over to Him. And then let go of it. Otherwise, the spirit of revenge could do more damage to us internally than anything anyone else could do to us externally.

DAY 27

When people ask you for something, give it to them.
When they want to borrow money, loan it to them.
                                              —*Matthew 5:42*

What do you feel when you approach a homeless person on the street? Or when a family stands by the side of the road with a cardboard sign reading, WILL WORK FOR FOOD? Or when a reputable service organization sends you an appeal to help?

Most of us experience a little bit of frustration and impatience, or sadness and helplessness, or perhaps even fear or anger. We worry about whether we should give. What if they misuse the money? What if they're lying?

Jesus would say, that's not your problem. Be obedient to His inner voice when an opportunity presents itself. Get as much information as you can, but be predisposed to give.

After all, think how much He gave you.

You have heard people say, "Love your neighbors and hate your enemies." But I tell you to love your enemies and pray for anyone who mistreats you.

—Matthew 5:43–44

Loving your neighbor is easy. And nobody ever said being Jesus' disciple would be easy.

His will is clear: Love and pray for your *enemies.*

Note that He isn't saying feel good about your enemies. Feelings have nothing to do with it.

It's a decision of your will, a decision to take positive action, to be proactive rather than reactive. And if that kind of behavior could become part of your lifestyle, before too long you may not have to keep doing it because you won't have any enemies.

You'll have only friends.

DAY 29

He makes the sun rise on both good and bad people. And he sends rain for the ones who do right and for the ones who do wrong.

—Matthew 5:45

Jesus has said in many ways to treat your friends and your enemies with equal compassion, love, and concern. After all, that's the way God operates. Both good and bad enjoy the sun and the rain.

And in the end, we can rest assured, it will all wash out.

Spend some time outdoors today, whether it's sunny or rainy, warm or chilly. Look around you. Whom do you see: Neighbors or strangers? Friends or enemies?

Pray for those you know and for those you don't. Commit before God to reach out to at least one of them in the next few days.

And be prepared to put into practice what Jesus has been telling you about how to relate to others.

DAY 30

If you love only those people who love you, will God reward you for that? Even tax collectors love their friends. If you greet only your friends, what's so great about that? Don't even unbelievers do that?

—Matthew 5:46–47

Few things in life feel better than being loved.

But Jesus says there is at least one thing: loving someone who doesn't love you. It gives you a reward nothing else can: the reward of loving as God Himself does.

Think it through. Put it into context. He isn't saying that you should be willing to put up with abuse or love in such a one-sided way that you're really doing it to meet your own needs. He's just saying, "Love."

Even the despised tax collectors of His day—who lived to cheat and extort from those they taxed—could handle loving someone who loved them back.

Thank God, you're different.

You must always act like your Father in heaven.
—*Matthew 5:48*

Wait a minute. Jesus seems to be setting a standard that's much higher than could ever make sense. Isn't He? After all, as the New King James puts it, "You shall be *perfect*."

Jesus is talking about loving others—whether friend or foe.

God's love is perfect and perfectly balanced. He sends sun and rain on the good and the bad.

And we—as His children, empowered by the Holy Spirit, encouraged by Jesus' example—are to seek to love as He does.

To reach out to anyone and everyone, anytime and everywhere.

Perfect love. It casts out fear. It's forgiving. It's energizing. It's freeing. And it's yours to experience every day of your life.

DAY 32

When you do good deeds, don't try to show off. If you do, you won't get a reward from your Father in heaven.

—Matthew 6:1

Motives. If they're wrong, they can undo everything.

Jesus asks us to examine our motives anytime we do good deeds. We give of our time, our concern, our love, our work, and our money. We listen compassionately when a friend calls to unload troubles. We volunteer to help at the shelter for homeless people. We call a congressperson on behalf of a family that has been wronged. We give to various causes that tug at our hearts.

Why? Is it to feel better about ourselves? Is it to gain some measure of acceptance or even praise from our peers? Is it to stifle for a while the self-message that we're not doing enough to be good enough? Is it to make God love us more? Or is it the natural outflow of a life in communion with the One who is all love . . . pure love . . . unlimited love?

Set your sights on that kind of love. Make it your goal for today.

DAY 33

When you give to the poor, don't let anyone know
about it. Then your gift will be given in secret. Your
Father knows what is done in secret, and he will reward you.

—Matthew 6:3–4

Nothing could be more fulfilling in life than to
be utterly unable to keep track of all the acts of
love we share—and not worry about it.

When we're centered in God, drawing continually on His refreshing resources, focused on
Him and not on ourselves, our lives can be glorious symphonies of charity. And we may not even
realize it.

Jesus promises us a reward from our Father
when we give of ourselves freely, humbly, and
honestly. Unfortunately, sometimes we feel guilty
knowing about that great reward. It makes us
wonder if our motive is gain.

But don't worry about that. Jesus wouldn't
have uttered this promise if He didn't want you
to believe it, act on it, and enjoy it eternally.

FEBRUARY 2

When you pray, go into a room alone and close the door. Pray to your Father in private. He knows what is done in private, and he will reward you.

—Matthew 6:6

Jesus had a real problem with religious ostentation, which was unfortunate for the leaders of His day because their whole religious life was built upon the wobbly—and ultimately false—foundation of pride and showiness.

Two thousand years later, the problem still plagues the church. And with the advent of high-tech communications and megachurches, it seems to be getting worse.

In this age of jam-packed schedules and crammed-in responsibilities, time alone with God—really alone—is a commodity more precious than gold.

But it can be yours for a small investment of a little time and a lot of humility.

The strange thing is, people who build their lives around times of solitude with God have an amazing ability to rearrange their priorities and schedules because they know it's worth it.

DAY 35

Your Father knows what you need before you ask.
—*Matthew 6:8*

It can be scary when someone else knows a deep, dark secret of yours. Perhaps you've confessed something to a friend, then later wondered nervously if the friend was really trustworthy enough. And perhaps you've experienced times when your fears were realized.

That's why it may be difficult to take comfort in Jesus' word today. Don't let it be disconcerting. Relax in it. And look at it for what it is: a promise that God knows everything about you. Every pain you feel. Every need that goes unmet. Every tear that runs down your face. Every hair you pull out in frustration. He knows far more about you than you do.

That's not to say you shouldn't tell Him how you feel and what you need. Thinking it through with Him in prayer enables you to maintain a completely honest relationship with Him. And it opens the door for Him to let you know what you really need.

FEBRUARY 4

DAY 36

You should pray like this: Our Father in heaven, help us to honor your name. Come and set up your kingdom, so that everyone on earth will obey you, as you are obeyed in heaven.

—*Matthew 6:9–10*

You may have repeated this prayer weekly or even daily throughout your life, which is all the more reason to spend time today taking these words one at a time, thinking them through meditatively.

Jesus never intended this prayer to be rote. It's not to be carved in stone and mindlessly uttered as some incantation. No, it's a living, breathing thing, a pattern for communication, an agenda to help you cover all the essentials in your prayer times. And it all centers on our Father, the holy One who rules and reigns in heaven and on earth—and in our lives.

Let these words be your invitation from Jesus today to worship the Father. Praise Him for who He is and what He is doing today. Let them be a springboard for an intimate conversation with your loving Abba.

DAY 37

Give us our food for today.
—Matthew 6:11

Jesus invites you to pray today for food. For your physical sustenance. For the necessities of life.

He makes it a simple, short, very direct request. There is no pleading involved. It's as if the mere asking for it guarantees it.

And so we take it for granted, particularly because it's unlikely that any of us have ever gone hungry for very long.

Just for today, refuse to take the physical graces of life—your food, water, air—for granted. Use each one as an occasion to thank Him. To pray for those who must plead for the necessities. And perhaps to do something more than pray for people who are hungry.

The Bread of Life Himself is ready to give you the strength and guidance you need to do just that.

DAY 38

Forgive our sins, as we forgive others.
—Matthew 6:12

Forgiveness can be exhilarating to receive and excruciating to give. But unless you forgive and are forgiven, you'll remain stuck in pain, guilt, and bitterness.

Jesus yearns for you to clear the air—and keep it clear—between you and God, and between you and everyone else. Life is too precious to let an unforgiving spirit drain it away.

Let forgiveness be a two-way street for you today—an avenue to a life of freedom. Ask God's Spirit to shine on your heart and expose the dark areas. Confess them. Turn away from them. Ask for His cleansing.

Then look at the bitternesses in your life where you have been wronged. And ask God to give you the strength to let them go and make them right.

Don't just say the words. Mean them. Do them. Live them.

DAY 39

Keep us from being tempted and protect us from evil.

—Matthew 6:13

Sometimes we get the attitude that God isn't fair. How in the world does He expect us to remain pure, holy, and clean in a world like ours?

We are bombarded by inducements to succumb to temptation. We steel ourselves, look the other way, but can't help feeling our minds are constantly being polluted.

Today, there's good news. God offers cleansing. Strength. Freedom. And His offer is backed by infinite power, glory, and authority. He has the right to give you what you need to stand strong, and He has the ability. What's more, He has the desire to do so.

The world really hasn't changed all that much, even since biblical times. It's just become more sophisticated in the ways it tempts.

Thank God, you can resist it. You can clothe yourself in His strength. You can yield to His loving protection.

DAY 40

If you forgive others for the wrongs they do to you, your Father in heaven will forgive you. But if you don't forgive others, your Father will not forgive your sins.

—*Matthew 6:14–15*

Jesus makes it clear that forgiveness is a serious affair. If you cannot forgive someone who has wronged you, you effectively cut off your fellowship with your Father in heaven. And until you make it right, it will only get worse.

Some say forgiveness is a foundation stone of the faith—God's forgiveness of each of us unto salvation. So unwillingness to forgive another proves the person is not a true disciple. This word from Jesus seems to validate that.

Perhaps you think you've forgiven. yet you keep grasping on to the hurts and the bitterness—sometimes years old. If you still feel the pain, you really haven't forgiven. Your mother, father, other family members, friends, coworkers, neighbors, employers, even strangers—all of them can hurt you deeply.

But thanks to the all-powerful One, you have the power to forgive them all today.

DAY 41

Don't store up treasures on earth! Moths and rust can destroy them, and thieves can break in and steal them. Instead, store up your treasures in heaven, where moths and rust cannot destroy them, and thieves cannot break in and steal them. Your heart will always be where your treasure is.

—*Matthew 6:19–21*

Every generation has had a problem with materialism. It's just that ours has a lot more material. Our televisions, newspapers, and magazines overflow with temptations to own, buy, and possess. We're flooded with opportunities to invest money with a goal to become independently wealthy and thereby content. Yet somehow, it all pales in the light of Jesus' words today because it all means nothing.

The flip side is to focus on heavenly treasures. They're indestructible. They can never be taken away. They'll bring joy and meaning forever.

Where have you set your heart? The world may have a lot to offer. But compare it to what God has in store for you. Now and forever.

Your eyes are like a window for your body. When they are good, you have all the light you need. But when your eyes are bad, everything is dark. If the light inside you is dark, you surely are in the dark.

—Matthew 6:22–23

Have you ever looked someone in the eyes and seen love? Have you looked and seen dark pain?

With a little spiritual discernment, you can tell a lot about how a person is doing by studying the eyes. They can veritably sparkle, or they can be utterly cloudy. They can be alert or sleepy. They can be bright or dark.

Jesus encourages you today to pay attention to the eyes of people you see. Their mouths may form a smile; their eyes may tell another story. He may give you an opportunity to minister to someone who needs a friend.

Before you do, take a good look at your eyes in a mirror. What do you see?

You cannot be the slave of two masters! You will like one more than the other or be more loyal to one than the other. You cannot serve both God and money.

—Matthew 6:24

Divided loyalties, hearts torn asunder. It's a battle each of us must fight, often daily. Hourly. Constantly.

Jesus' word is simple and direct: You can't serve God and money. Either demands total authority.

That's not to say that money is evil or that you shouldn't own things. Elsewhere Jesus is clear about the importance of stewardship of money and possessions. It all comes down to your purpose in wanting things. Is it to soothe an old pain? To try to fulfill someone else's idea of success? To be better than a neighbor? Or just to feel good?

If so, these desires will never be satisfied. Because only one of the masters—God or money—has the power to satisfy genuinely. So for today, which is it for you?

DAY 44

I tell you not to worry about your life. Don't worry about having something to eat, drink, or wear. Isn't life more than food or clothing?

—Matthew 6:25

Life is filled with little worries that gnaw away at our wholeness. The unexpected bills. The little bugs we catch that slow us down. Plans that go awry. Situations that goad us into feeling incomplete or discontented. Loneliness.

Sometimes we allow the little worries to become gigantic and dominate our thoughts, overtake our lives, and strangle our freedom.

When we get in that place, we feel virtually unable to stop worrying. In fact, Jesus' words can sound terribly simplistic.

But that's because His is a simple faith. And we keep wanting to complicate it.

Jesus offers simple freedom. Life is too much fun to waste it in worrying. Let Him show you how it can work today.

Look at the birds in the sky! They don't plant or harvest. They don't even store grain in barns. Yet your Father in heaven takes care of them. Aren't you worth more than birds?

—Matthew 6:26

You are of infinite value to God. Bask for a few moments in that thought.

He will care for your every need. He will listen to you when you call. He will lift you up in His love. He will carry you through the dark times. He will protect you in the midst of storms. He will invite you into His mothering nest. He will feed you with spiritual nourishment as you seek it. He will keep you warm.

Why do we doubt that? Why are we of so little value to ourselves? Why do we assume we are of little value to others? Or to God?

God cares for you—no matter how you feel or what you've done. He knows you thoroughly. He loves you.

To Jesus, that loving care was self-evident. It can be for you today as well.

DAY 46

Can worry make you live longer?
—Matthew 6:27

Worrying wastes time. It has no productive value.

But don't confuse worry with constructive thinking and healthy self-analysis. Sometimes these mind activities can turn into worry, pure and simple. That's a trap Jesus would encourage us to avoid falling into.

What's been on your mind in recent days? Struggles with your family? Conflict in an important relationship? A financial squeeze? A decision you must make? A loved one's illness? A shaky job situation? An uncertain future? It seems the mind never lacks for something to worry about.

Step back from the situations, and look carefully at how you're dealing with them. Are you obsessing endlessly about them, or are you taking time here and there to think them through, ponder your options, set them aside in God's hands, and let whatever happens happen?

Jesus invites you to shut off your worry and trust Him.

FEBRUARY 15

DAY 47

But more than anything else, put God's work first and do what he wants. Then all the other things will be yours as well.

—Matthew 6:33

Food, clothing, shelter. The basic necessities of life. We work hard to get them, so they take much of our time and attention.

To meet the basic needs, you and/or your spouse work. It may be an eight-hour day, but it consumes far more time and energy.

Many people let work become the fulcrum of their lives. They let themselves become overwhelmed by the responsibilities. They keep trying to work up and up for more prestige and bigger paychecks. The job becomes the most important part of their lives, to the detriment of family, friends, and faith.

Today, Jesus shakes up our priorities. One thing is worthy of our yearning, our seeking. God's work, His kingdom on earth, His righteous way of living, His relationship with you.

When that's well established, everything else falls into proper perspective.

Don't worry about tomorrow. It will take care of itself. You have enough to worry about today.
—Matthew 6:34

You've got enough to think about today without getting all tangled up in the future. There's
plenty of trouble today to keep you busy.

We can smile about that word of advice for
today because we know it's true. And time and
time again, we're forced to remind ourselves to
take life one day at a time.

Sometimes you may wish God would let you
know what's around the corner in the path of
your life. Wouldn't it make things so much easier
to know so you could relax and coast through it?

But when you realize how you would have felt
a year ago if you had known everything that was
about to happen the next year, you'll probably
acknowledge that it would have been overwhelming.

The future is in God's hands, right where it
belongs. Today is His gift to you to work
through, experience, and enjoy. And that's
enough for now.

Don't condemn others, and God will not condemn you. God will be as hard on you as you are on others! He will treat you exactly as you treat them.

—Matthew 7:1–2

When you're the one being condemned or judged, it's easy to agree with this word from Jesus. After all, who has a right to tell you how to think and act and live? Only God.

But beware, because that very attitude is judgmental, too. He will treat you in the same manner you treat others.

If you are in relationship with God, open to His leading, honest in your communication with Him, that's all you need to do. Don't worry about anyone else. And if others are concerned about you, don't let their judgmental attitude rub you the wrong way.

Reconciliation is the flip side of condemnation. And the God who reconciled the world to Himself is ready to help you follow His example.

You can see the speck in your friend's eye, but you don't notice the log in your own eye. How can you say, "My friend, let me take the speck out of your eye," when you don't see the log in your own eye? You're nothing but showoffs! First, take the log out of your own eye. Then you can see how to take the speck out of your friend's eye.

—Matthew 7:3–5

Jesus is having a little fun with us today. It's a hilarious scene; unfortunately, it possesses the sting of truth. He reminds us to remind ourselves that any time a judgmental thought pops into our minds, we ought to grab a mirror. We ought to build the habit of examining our hearts and motives when we start examining someone else's.

That is not easy to do. And because we have a log in our eye, we're blind to our need to deal with our problem.

But notice that once we take care of our situation, Jesus encourages us to approach a brother or sister in loving concern to help with the painful eye speck.

Ask, and you will receive. Search, and you will find. Knock, and the door will be opened for you. Everyone who asks will receive. Everyone who searches will find. And the door will be opened for everyone who knocks.

—Matthew 7:7–8

God knows what we need and what we want. But somehow, He likes it when we ask for it. Otherwise, we may get stuck in our neediness and our wanting. We may become superfocused on ourselves. The process of asking, searching, knocking for what we need opens the door for Him to enter and move. It restores the flow of our lives.

But notice, Jesus isn't guaranteeing you'll get what you want. All He's saying is, if you ask, you'll receive—something. It may be something else entirely. It may be that you receive the loss of that particular desire. Or it may indeed be what you had in mind all along.

Our confidence is that God knows best. And when we ask for His will in our lives, He will give it in abundance. Even today.

Would any of you give your hungry child a stone, if the child asked for some bread? Would you give your child a snake if the child asked for a fish? As bad as you are, you still know how to give good gifts to your children. But your heavenly Father is even more ready to give good things to people who ask.

—Matthew 7:9–11

Your heavenly Father is infinitely willing to give you all good things—if only you will ask!

Jesus offers examples of how a human parent would give whatever the child asks to meet needs. A parent would never give something that would hurt the child. And in comparison to God, human parents are bad, Jesus says!

"Your heavenly Father," Jesus says, "is even more ready to give good things." Sometimes that's hard to believe. But perhaps that's because we're so used to not asking for what we want.

What do you want? What do you need? What are you willing to ask for today?

DAY 53

Treat others as you want them to treat you. This is what the Law and the Prophets are all about.

—*Matthew 7:12*

The golden rule. Here Jesus says it summarizes the entire Old Testament.

Put some thought around it. What do you want people to do for you?

You want them to listen to you when you need to talk. Befriend you. Reach out to you when you need a touch. Support you when you're burdened. Pray for you. Talk with you. Encourage you. Confront you lovingly when necessary. Give something special to you. Care about you. Share with you. Respect you. Allow you to be you. Accept the way you are. Maintain healthy limits with you. Love you.

Think about the people in your life. Is anyone doing these things for you? Who?

Now think through the lists again. Which of these things have you been doing for others? How many people are you relating to this way?

Finally, read Jesus' words again, and ask Him to help you put them to work today.

Go in through the narrow gate. The gate to destruction is wide, and the road that leads there is easy to follow. A lot of people go through that gate. But the gate to life is very narrow. The road that leads there is so hard to follow that only a few people find it.

—Matthew 7:13–14

It's not easy being a follower of Christ. The way is narrow and difficult. And often it seems there are few others on the path with you. But consider the alternative: destruction.

If the path you've chosen to walk seems too easy, perhaps you're not walking fast enough. Or perhaps you haven't chosen the right path yet.

Narrow as it might be, there's always room on the path for Jesus to walk with you. To hold your hand when you grow weary. To let you run ahead a little way on your own. Or even to carry you when you can go no farther.

Take a walk today, and use it as an opportunity to talk to Him about where you are on the path.

Watch out for false prophets! They dress up like sheep, but inside they are wolves who have come to attack you. You can tell what they are by what they do.

—Matthew 7:15–16

You can't judge a wolf by his clothing. Wait and see what he does and how he lives.

There is an often overwhelming amount of nonsense, misunderstanding, falsehood, and even evil passed off as legitimate pathways to God. New doctrines, innovative methods, and unique concepts abound in a society that hungers for truth and personal peace. We grope for new experiences to rekindle our spirits.

There is no shortage of false prophets, wolves in sheep's clothing. And yet, with the preponderance of new approaches, does anything really change? No.

Be discerning today. Ask the Holy Spirit for wisdom. And ask Him to help you live your life to show the world that His way is the only way that fulfills.

Not everyone who calls me their Lord will get into the kingdom of heaven. Only the ones who obey my Father in heaven will get in.

—Matthew 7:21

Words are meaningless if they're not backed by actions. And the actions are meaningless unless they are the Father's will.

We all know of people—on a personal basis and in the public eye—whose authenticity we may doubt. They may look good, say the right things, but something doesn't ring true.

Don't think about them today. They are not your concern. You are.

Sometimes it may seem you don't mean what you're saying or doing as His follower. But times like these are not what Jesus has in mind. He's talking about a lack of a genuine, living, working faith.

Today, take the opportunity to examine your words, your deeds, your motives, and your desire to do His will.

Anyone who hears and obeys these teachings of mine is like a wise person who built a house on solid rock. Rain poured down, rivers flooded, and winds beat against that house. But it did not fall, because it was built on solid rock.

—*Matthew 7:24–25*

The whole purpose of this book of meditations is to enable Jesus' words to confront you daily. And today's verses tell you why that's important.

Jesus didn't mince words or simply air opinions. His words carry weight. In fact, they're the rock on which we can build our lives in confidence and security.

It's one thing to read Jesus' words. It's another thing to think them through, consider what they mean to you personally. But it's yet another thing entirely to do them. That's a lifelong challenge. But accepting that challenge is the wisest choice you could ever make.

How firm is your foundation? How shaky does your life feel? When you answer these questions, you'll know what foundation you're building on.

I do want to! Now you are well.
—*Matthew 8:3*

One of the outcasts of society approached the Master. The man with leprosy worshipfully, respectfully, yet directly said to Him, "Lord, you have the power to make me well, if only you wanted to."

The law forbade touching a person with leprosy. But Jesus put out His hand and did just that. After all, the law of love is foremost.

Jesus said, "I do want to! Now you are well." And immediately, the man was freed of his malady. He was clean and new and free and alive.

Today, Jesus wants to answer a prayer for cleansing: physically, emotionally, and spiritually. Are you willing to ask Him directly for it?

Prepare yourself for His cleansing touch.

Then Jesus said to the officer, "You may go home now. Your faith has made it happen." Right then his servant was healed.

—Matthew 8:13

He was not even a Jew but a Roman officer. Still, he serves as an example of unyielding faith in God, for he approached the Lord on behalf of a paralyzed, tormented servant at his home.

Jesus immediately offered to go to heal the servant. But the officer would have none of it: "Lord, I'm not good enough for you to come into my house. Just give the order, and my servant will get well."

Jesus marveled. Never before, even among His own people, had He encountered such faith. And that faith made the difference.

The officer's faith startled the Lord with its boldness. And it brought forth a miracle. Are you seeing miracles like that in your life? Are you living a life of faith like that?

Foxes have dens, and birds have nests. But the Son of Man does not have a place to call his own.
—*Matthew 8:20*

A Jewish leader approached Jesus to tell Him, "I'll go anywhere with you!"

Apparently, Jesus could see through the rash commitment. His words in reply indicated a price must be paid to follow Him.

In those days, that price was literal. Today, we don't have to leave our homes and families to follow Jesus wherever He traveled. He's here. He's everywhere. But the cost remains.

Jesus was willing to forgo the pleasures of possessions and place. He may not be calling you to that today. But He is reminding you of the sacrifices His children will pay to be free enough to follow Him wherever He leads.

What sacrifices are you making? What sacrifices are you willing to make? These are important questions to ask about your relationship with the One who made the ultimate sacrifice for you.

DAY 61

Come with me, and let the dead bury their dead.
—*Matthew 8:22*

Family matters press on us. Responsibilities loom over us. The to-do list grows endlessly. We manage to keep busy trying to get all the little things out of the way, so we can focus on the top priorities. But the little things reproduce exponentially. The top priorities get transferred to the wish list where they languish until finally, we forget we ever had those priorities in the first place.

What is your top priority? Verbalize it. Write it. Ask yourself how much time you devote daily to fulfilling that priority. Ask yourself if it's an appropriate top priority. Why?

What is Jesus suggesting should be your top priority? What can you do today to make that your top priority in deed as well as in word? Ask Jesus to help you answer that question.

Why are you so afraid? You surely don't have much faith.

—Matthew 8:26

The disciples were frantic, certain of a watery doom in the stormy lake.

And Jesus just slept.

What kind of Savior was that? As it turned out, a powerful one. He chided His closest friends for being frightened, then calmed the deadly storm with a word.

Their fear made no sense to Him. After all, He was the King of the universe. All authority was His. And He was in their midst. What were a few raindrops to Him?

Do you ever hear Jesus saying these words to you? Your faith is potentially powerful because your faith is in the same Person who stilled the storm.

People, jobs, events, illness—there are plenty of reasons to fear today.

But your Savior is not sleeping now. He is fully aware of your fears. And He is ready and willing to calm them. Just ask.

DAY 63

With one word from Jesus, a horde of evil spirits left two helpless men to inhabit a herd of pigs, which then ran headlong into the lake to their deaths.

One word. One command: Go.

The authority of Jesus is limitless. Nothing can withstand His power. He is the Lord indeed.

The demons had no alternative but to obey Him. You, on the other hand, have a choice because God created you with a will. The Bible makes it clear that obedience can bring fulfillment and blessing, and disobedience will bring consequences and pain. Still, the choice is yours.

Every day you read this book, you face a choice. To hear or to tune out. To obey or to ignore. To follow or to stand still.

Today, thank God that He has given you the power to choose. Then, make your choice wisely.

My friend, don't worry! Your sins are forgiven.
—Matthew 9:2

A paralyzed man was brought to the Savior, who had compassion on him. And His words of healing were words of forgiveness.

The man's sins had tied him up to the point of physical disability. He was frozen in pain. Bent. Broken. Helpless.

Until Jesus spoke these words. Don't worry! Your sins no longer have power over you. And the man was set free—physically as well as spiritually.

Today, Jesus extends the same power of forgiveness to you. As a believer, you have trusted Him to take your sins away. But you may still be holding on to their paralyzing consequences. Frozen in your ability to live and move in Him. Incapable of reaching out to others in healthy, life-giving ways. You, too, may at times feel bent, broken, and helpless. Listen as Jesus speaks the words of forgiveness to you today.

But Jesus knew what was in their minds, and he said, "Why are you thinking such evil things? Is it easier for me to tell this crippled man that his sins are forgiven or to tell him to get up and walk? But I will show you that the Son of Man has the right to forgive sins here on earth." So Jesus said to the man, "Get up! Pick up your mat and go on home."

—Matthew 9:4–6

The religious leaders were shocked that Jesus would claim the authority to forgive sins. Swiftly, He attacked them for their evil intentions and defended His actions. Then, to prove His authority over sin, He commanded the paralyzed man to stand up. The people gathered around must have been stunned—either in rage or in adoration—as the power to forgive sins was demonstrated physically before their very eyes.

This same Jesus is alive today. He is with you in power and love. He has forgiven your sins. And He commands you to arise. Stand up, and shake off the emotional and spiritual paralysis that keeps you from being fully free to follow Him.

Come with me.

—Matthew 9:9

Jesus approached a man who was almost universally disliked, if not despised, by the people he collected taxes from.

And He saw Matthew for the follower that He was.

The invitation was extended—simply, directly. It was actually a command. And Matthew the tax collector responded immediately.

He left his office to be with a Man he didn't know, to do things and go places that were beyond his ability to imagine.

Picture yourself as Matthew. What draws you to follow this Man? What is it about Him that prompts you to obey immediately? What emotions do you feel as you leave your office?

Jesus is extending the invitation to you.

Arise.

Healthy people don't need a doctor, but sick people do. Go and learn what the Scriptures mean when they say, "Instead of offering sacrifices to me, I want you to be merciful to others." I did not come to invite good people to be my followers. I came to invite sinners.

—*Matthew 9:12–13*

The religious leaders question Jesus' motives for eating with tax collectors and sinners. But they need Him most, and Jesus rebukes the leaders who painstakingly followed the minutiae of the law while conveniently ignoring its heart of love and grace.

Jesus came to offer aid and comfort. To extend God's mercy even to persons considered social outcasts. To be the Physician for soulsick people.

The religious leaders may have thought they were well, but they weren't. We must acknowledge our need before the Physician can heal.

DAY 68

The friends of a bridegroom don't go without eating
while he is still with them. But the time will come
when he will be taken from them. Then they will go
without eating.

—Matthew 9:15

Clearly, Jesus and His followers were having
too much fun. They were reveling in the glory of
acceptance and love and community. And they
were living the life of freedom that comes from
following Jesus wholeheartedly.

Jesus admitted to the sober followers of John
the Baptist that it wouldn't last. He would be
taken away. But life would continue.

In the meantime, it was party time. The
Bridegroom was the host and all were invited.

Life is a series of parties and fasts and all things
in between. Today, you may be fasting spiritually
if not physically. If so, you may not realize you've
been invited to a party. It may be with fellow
brothers and sisters, or it may be in your soul.
Jesus, your Host, awaits your presence.

MARCH 8

No one uses a new piece of cloth to patch old clothes. The patch would shrink and tear a bigger hole. No one pours new wine into old wineskins. The wine would swell and burst the old skins. Then the wine would be lost, and the skins would be ruined. New wine must be put into new wineskins. Both the skins and the wine will then be safe.

—Matthew 9:16–17

Jesus offers a totally new way of life. One founded on the concept of grace rather than legalism. One that is as flexible as new cloth or leather. One that is truly alive with passion, pain, and joy.

A lifestyle like this can't be patched on to a set of empty, brittle, confining, and obsolete rules. It's new wine for the soul.

If you're struggling with trying to make the pieces fit in your life, your struggle is useless. Give Jesus the pieces today. All of them. And He'll give you something totally new in return.

Don't worry. You are now well because of your faith.
—*Matthew 9:22*

According to her religion, her flow of blood made the woman unclean. She was not to be touched, or her uncleanness would spread. For twelve years, she had suffered not only from the physical malady but also from the ostracism.

Then Jesus came. He was on His way to another place when the woman—hesitantly in one sense, yet boldly in another—reached out to touch the hem of His garment. In faith.

The woman took the initiative and reached out to the Savior. And her faith made her well. It was a simple gesture on her part, but it cataclysmically changed her life because the gesture was a reach toward Jesus.

Today, follow her example. Overcome whatever imprisonment you find yourself in by reaching out for Jesus.

Get out of here! The little girl is not dead. She is just asleep.

—Matthew 9:24

They were professional mourners gathered at the ruler's home to weep and wail over his daughter's untimely death. It was just a job.

The Man worked His way through the crowd, saying something that made absolutely no sense: The girl wasn't dead after all.

The mourners laughed. They ridiculed Him. The Man was nuts!

The mourners were hustled outside the house. Undoubtedly, their wailing and flute playing had been silenced. Then Jesus took the girl by her hand, and she arose.

You see, Jesus knows what He's talking about. But too often we become so hardened by what we see, so trapped in our small understanding of life, so bound up in the way we live our lives, that we really don't take Him seriously. At such times Jesus loves to surprise us.

Prepare yourself to be surprised today.

[Jesus] asked them, "Do you believe I can make you well?" "Yes, Lord," they answered. Jesus touched their eyes and said, "Because of your faith, you will be healed."

—Matthew 9:28–29

Two blind men heard the commotion that arose when Jesus raised a little girl from death. So when Jesus left that house, they followed Him, crying out after Him, "Son of David, have pity on us!" And they kept after Him, all the way into the house He entered.

A question, an answer, a touch: "Because of your faith, you will be healed."

The men had proved their hopes by persisting in following Him. They had validated their faith verbally. But it was still to be determined whether their faith in Jesus was genuine.

Jesus makes it clear that our faith has much to do with the outcome of our lives. He is quite capable of healing and empowering if we ask Him in faith.

What do you want Him to do in your life today? He's ready. Are you?

DAY 73

A large crop is in the fields, but there are only a few workers. Ask the Lord in charge of the harvest to send out workers to bring it in.

—*Matthew 9:37–38*

These words of Jesus have inspired countless believers to sacrifice their home comforts and spread the gospel as missionaries. But sometimes we forget why Jesus said them to His disciples.

Jesus was traveling from town to town, teaching, ministering, healing. The crowd that followed Him grew ever larger. As He looked out on the multitude, His heart overflowed with compassion: "They were confused and helpless, like sheep without a shepherd" (Matt. 9:36).

Today, He looks at you with compassion and care. His touch on your life is available to you.

The world is filled with hungry, hurting people not just overseas but in your own neighborhood. You can look around you at the weary multitude in your midst and share His compassion with them.

DAY 74

As you go, announce that the kingdom of heaven will soon be here.

—Matthew 10:7

Jesus sends His closest friends out into the countryside with a mission: Tell others that "the kingdom of heaven will soon be here." It's here, ready to be experienced by people who are ready.

As a believer, you are a citizen of God's kingdom. You are part of God's economy—His way of living—here on earth. And until you enter the eternal, heavenly kingdom, you are His ambassador where you are.

You may attract others to join you if you cry out, "The kingdom of heaven will soon be here." But today, you may have a far deeper impact on other people's lives by living and serving as though you were already in His kingdom. Because you are.

Talk to your King about how you can serve as His herald, His ambassador, His foreign minister today.

Heal the sick, raise the dead to life, heal people who have leprosy, and force out demons. You received without paying, now give without being paid.

—Matthew 10:8

Jesus instructs His disciples what to do when they go forth into the world as His representatives. And He makes performing miracles sound positively easy.

To the disciples' surprise, they had a profound impact on many lives—physically, spiritually, and emotionally.

How did that happen? Jesus gives the answer: "You received without paying, now give without being paid."

God doesn't wish to put any restrictions on the blessings and the power He bestows on His children. He gives freely, without reservation.

But it's for a purpose. Not to make us feel powerful. Not to make us feel superior. But to make us servants who give freely, without expecting anything in return.

When you go to a home, give it your blessing of peace. If the home is deserving, let your blessing remain with them. But if the home is not deserving, take back your blessing of peace.

—*Matthew 10:12–13*

Wherever you go, let your peace go there, too. Extend God's peace when you go into a home. Or a workplace. Or a hospital. Or a church.

As a follower of Jesus, indwelt by Him, you carry His peace with you. You may not always feel it, but it's there, ready for you to draw on. And when you draw on it personally, you can extend it to others.

But Jesus advises His disciples to be discerning. And if they enter a place that is not deserving of His peace, just keep it to themselves.

His peace is a valuable commodity. Of course, there's an infinite supply of it. It's just not to be wasted where it wouldn't be appreciated.

With His spirit of discernment, go about your day looking for places to spread peace.

I am sending you like lambs into a pack of wolves. So be as wise as snakes and as innocent as doves.

—Matthew 10:16

The world can be a vicious place, filled with ravenous wolves that seek to tear at the souls of the sheep of God.

Jesus sent out His disciples into such a place. Not to be sheepish, but to be His sheep under His compassionate care.

They had to be ready for anything. Harassment, injury, perhaps even death. Therefore, Jesus said, "Be as wise as snakes and as innocent as doves." In other words, be innocent—sincere, direct, and honest—and also wise—aware, smart, and savvy.

It's a good idea to be aware of how the world operates and be on your guard against it. But it's also important to cause no offense.

The word pictures of being like snakes and doves seem contradictory. But both are true. Which aspect do you need to work on today? Ask God to give you an opportunity to practice.

But when someone arrests you, don't worry about what you will say or how you will say it. At that time you will be given the words to say. But you will not really be the one speaking. The Spirit from your Father will tell you what to say.

—Matthew 10:19–20

Jesus' disciples faced opposition not only from the government but also from religious leaders. The same is true even today for Christians in many parts of the world.

Jesus calls us to love. That's radical. That's risky. It means doing things some people won't approve of—even some "Christians." It means taking active stands many won't agree with.

Plan to do something radically loving today for others. Visit a hospice or a soup kitchen, and ask how you can get involved. Let God prod your desire and your enthusiasm as you reach out. But prepare yourself to rely on Him to speak through you to give a defense.

Brothers and sisters will betray one another and have each other put to death. Parents will betray their own children, and children will turn against their parents and have them killed. Everyone will hate you because of me. But if you remain faithful until the end, you will be saved.

—Matthew 10:21–22

Jesus pulls no punches about the impact that genuine faith can make in our lives. And it's not a pretty picture—at least on the surface.

Death! At the hands of brothers, sisters, parents, and children? All for the sake of Jesus?

It's a warning that may be hard for us to relate to. But it indicates just how radical and revolutionary faith can be—and perhaps should be.

You may be faced with severe opposition. And in those cases, Jesus encourages you to endure.

Stand firm. Be strong in His power. Rest in Him in total confidence. And fear not, because it will all work out in the end.

Disciples are not better than their teacher, and slaves are not better than their master. It is enough for disciples to be like their teacher and for slaves to be like their master.

—Matthew 10:24–25

Disciple. Slave. That's what you are.

Teacher. Master. That's what Jesus is.

Read these words of Jesus, and they seem to make obvious sense—of course we're not above our Master. But when Jesus said these words, He was speaking of the persecution He faced. The hatred. And even death. And He's saying, in effect, don't expect to get any better treatment than He received. You're not above getting that kind of treatment from this world.

Our goal as disciples of Jesus is to be like Him, our Teacher. Our goal as slaves is to be like our Master.

Spend a few moments considering how close you're becoming to these goals today.

Don't be afraid of anyone! Everything that is hidden will be found out, and every secret will be known.
—*Matthew 10:26*

You shouldn't fear those of this world who are antagonistic toward the way of the cross. They have no power, ultimately, over you.

In fact, Jesus says, there will come a day when every evil deed of people who persecuted His children will be brought into the light of God's judgment.

Nothing will remain hidden. And God's judgment of the evil ones will be sure.

Yet fear often grips our hearts when we're forced to take a stand or say a word on behalf of our Lord at work, to a neighbor or friend, or wherever we may find ourselves in the world.

We fear a disapproving smirk. Perhaps a snide word. Worse, an intellectual challenge that we may not be up to. We really don't know what persecution is, do we?

Stand tall. Your Savior is worth the risk. And He will be with you all the way.

Whatever I say to you in the dark, you must tell in the light. And you must announce from the house-tops whatever I have whispered to you.

—Matthew 10:27

*B*old. *Enthusiastic. Bright. Joyful. Excited. Courageous.*

Are these words that others would apply to your life today? They're words that could describe Jesus' followers who take His words here to heart.

The Savior tells His disciples to tell others boldly what He has told them privately, in the dark, with whispers. To take to heart His promise to be with them always. To be utterly confident in His power and provision. To be free enough to shout His love and grace from the housetops.

Today, Jesus' command to His disciples may be difficult for you to hear. If so, be quiet a few moments. Let Him whisper to you in the dark. Let Him assure you of His love for you, His desire to help you become stronger. Tomorrow may be a better day to climb out on the housetop.

DAY 83

Don't be afraid of people. They can kill you, but they cannot harm your soul. Instead, you should fear God who can destroy both your body and your soul in hell.

—Matthew 10:28

When it comes to eternity, if you've made your choice for God, you've made the right choice—although it may not seem right in the face of difficulties or persecution.

Jesus promises that no harm can ever come to the soul of one of God's children. It will live forever. The body, however, is not so fortunate. But your soul is the real you, not your body. So anyone who threatens you with physical harm is really not threatening you.

By contrast, God has ultimate authority over the souls of those who choose not to follow Him. That, too, has eternal consequences.

The point is, you're in good hands. They're the hands that formed the universe. The hands that keep it running. The hands that possess all authority forever.

The hands that hold you as a father holds a child.

Aren't two sparrows sold for only a penny? But your Father knows when any one of them falls to the ground. Even the hairs on your head are counted. So don't be afraid! You are worth much more than many sparrows.

—Matthew 10:29–31

Doesn't God care that your finances are straining you to the breaking point? Doesn't God care that the friction in your closest relationship is getting to the point of impossibility? Doesn't God care that your loneliness at times overwhelms you with its darkness? Doesn't God care that your mind is reeling over the decision you're facing? Yes. Yes. Yes. Yes. And forever yes.

God knows every ache you feel. Every glimmer of hope that bubbles up. Every little fear that pinches your soul. Every hair on your head. And more than that, He cares about it. His goal is to see you become all you possibly can be as a human being on earth.

If you tell others that you belong to me, I will tell my Father in heaven that you are my followers. But if you reject me, I will tell my Father in heaven that you don't belong to me.

—*Matthew 10:32–33*

Jesus has a problem with secret disciples. Followers of His who really don't want to advertise the part. Followers who skulk to their churches on Sunday morning but keep their faith hidden throughout the week. Followers who, faced with an opportunity to share a word of peace and encouragement or to perform an act of love and concern, instead turn their eyes away from the need. Followers who deny Him by denying their need to grow spiritually and emotionally, and stay stuck and stagnant where they are.

Jesus says there are consequences for living this way.

On the other hand, there are great rewards for living a transparently Christian life.

Examine yourself today in light of Jesus' words. And don't keep Him a secret.

Don't think that I came to bring peace to the earth!
I came to bring trouble, not peace.

—Matthew 10:34

These are jarring words of Jesus. We like to think of Him exclusively as the Peacemaker. The calmer of all storms. The settler of all disputes. The healer of all relational wounds. The balm for a life of frustration. He can be all these things. And surely, He has been all these things in your life at one time or another.

But today, He acknowledges that His distinctly different way of life, His revolutionary perspective on life's priorities, and His unique purposes for His children will naturally set up differences. And difficulties. And even divisions. And these divisions are important enough to stand our ground for.

Today, you can take some measure of encouragement from Jesus, who tells you problems are to be expected when you live out your faith. You can love in the midst of troubles. Keep trying to do that today.

If you love your father or mother or even your sons and daughters more than me, you are not fit to be my disciples.

—Matthew 10:37

Jesus sets up clear priorities for His children. And He allows no slack: He is to come first in our lives. Even above our parents. Even above our own children.

When we get tied up in other relationships, whether healthy or not, we can become totally focused on them and leave Jesus on the periphery.

Jesus is saying, take Him with you in all your dealings with loved ones.

You may be feeling that your problem with your father or mother or son or daughter is not that you love too much because you're experiencing deep pain in the relationship—and perhaps it's old pain.

Even so, listen to Jesus. Don't become distracted by the way things are. Focus on Him first. Open yourself to Him totally. Let go of your pain and fears. And He will be with you in all your relationships.

And unless you are willing to take up your cross and come with me, you are not fit to be my disciples.

—Matthew 10:38

In Jesus' society, the cross was a symbol of death. It was the barbaric method of capital punishment used by the Romans—the method Jesus Himself would eventually experience on our behalf.

He says, take up your cross. That's more than carrying a difficult burden. It's more than bearing your pain and suffering. It's death. But it's life.

It's a genuine willingness to put your entire life on the line for your Lord. And it's the first step to really following Jesus.

Jesus says very plainly that it's not an option Unless you're willing to sacrifice your life—and everything you hold dear—you're not really following Him.

Where does Jesus fit in the mix of who you are? Now you know where He wants to be.

If you try to save your life, you will lose it. But if you give it up for me, you will surely find it.

—Matthew 10:39

There are many paradoxes in the life of faith, and this is one of them.

Jesus says that in discovering genuine life, life with Him, you will lose life, life as you now know it.

The life you are exchanging is self-focused, weak, empty, and powerless. It is but a shadow of what is possible, of what is promised.

Losing that life—submitting it in openhanded faith to God—is the doorway to finding a far better life. A life that offers comfort, encouragement, and growth even in the midst of struggles and pain. A life that over time becomes increasingly giving because internal resources have increased. A life that becomes richer and more fulfilling day by day.

Today, that kind of life is within your grasp.

Anyone who welcomes you welcomes me. And anyone who welcomes me also welcomes the one who sent me.

—Matthew 10:40

People who follow Jesus—including you—serve as His representatives wherever they go. You take Him with you, no matter where you are. So those with whom you have contact are in reality making contact with Jesus Himself.

The relationships are powerful. You bring Jesus; Jesus brings the totality of God to human experience. When you are welcomed, Jesus is welcomed, and the Father is welcomed, too.

Jesus is with you today to protect and encourage you. To strengthen you in the face of difficulty or opposition. To give you wisdom in the way you reach out to others. To offer love through you.

Perhaps you didn't realize you had such an awesome traveling companion.

Anyone who welcomes a prophet, just because that person is a prophet, will be given the same reward as a prophet. Anyone who welcomes a good person, just because that person is good, will be given the same reward as a good person.

—*Matthew 10:41*

Be open to God. Be willing to extend a welcome. Be discerning. Be ready.

Jesus says that welcoming one of God's people will bring reward. And the reward is God Himself. His presence. His truth. His assurance.

Unfortunately, we've become spiritually suspicious people. We fear being duped, misled, abused. And rightly so.

But there have always been spiritual swindlers in our midst. That's why we need to depend on God's Spirit within us to discern a true prophet.

Trust the Spirit. Then open yourself to whatever God would bring your way. Welcome Him, and be richly rewarded.

And whoever gives one of these little ones only a cup of cold water in the name of a disciple, assuredly, I say to you, he shall by no means lose his reward.

—*Matthew 10:42 NKJV*

An act of mercy offered in the name of Jesus is a powerful experience.

But Jesus says offering a cup of cool water even in the name of one of His disciples is just as powerful because He is one with His followers.

That's a compelling thought. It balances Jesus' power and presence with His humility in working through our clay vessels.

It shows His willingness to put up with the obvious hindrances to working through us—our stubbornness, our suspicions, our sin.

And it also demonstrates how simple it can be to "be Jesus" to someone in need. A cup of cool water. A loving touch. An open ear. Simple ways to bring the Savior to a needy soul today.

Let them spur your heart to be ready to serve in Jesus' name.

If you have ears, pay attention!
—*Matthew 11:15*

Jesus said these words many times to people who gathered around Him, listening. It was a way to tell them, "Listen up! This is important." But more than that, it recognized that some people are ready to hear and to obey. And others are not.

Jesus' words are often obscure. He spoke in parables to illustrate His point. His confused disciples would often ask Him, "What did You mean when You told that story?" And He would explain it for them.

They wanted to hear, to understand, and to live in light of what Jesus had said. They had ears and paid attention.

Jesus wants open ears. Understanding minds. Obedient hearts. Individuals who are so inclined will truly hear and be amazed.

Right now, be quiet. Let go of your preconceived notions. Listen expectantly. Jesus is speaking to you.

My Father, Lord of heaven and earth, I am grateful that you hid all this from wise and educated people and showed it to ordinary people. Yes, Father, that is what pleased you.

—Matthew 11:25–26

God the Father, the Lord of heaven and earth, knows what He's doing. We can be confident of that. And one of the things He's doing is keeping the truth that Jesus reveals from "wise and educated people"—at least those who are wise and educated in their own eyes.

In Jesus' day, it was the religious leaders. They had great knowledge and understanding in their heads, but their hearts were devoid of genuine devotion and mercy.

Jesus chose instead to work through those who were open to Him and His revolutionary word. He calls them "ordinary people." And that pleased the Father.

All of earth's wisdom fades into nothingness before the truth Jesus revealed. Today, come to Him. He's waiting for you.

My Father has given me everything, and he is the only one who knows the Son. The only one who truly knows the Father is the Son. But the Son wants to tell others about the Father, so that they can know him too.

—*Matthew 11:27*

Jesus alone has a relationship of absolute intimacy with the Father. Nothing can come between them. So everything He said and did while He was on earth revealed the Father to us as nothing else could.

It's God's desire that His children know Him intimately. He desires that we experience Him totally. And that can happen through His Son, our Savior, Jesus Christ.

What has Jesus been revealing to you about the Father? About His desire for you? He yearns to share those things with you today.

If you are tired from carrying heavy burdens, come to me and I will give you rest.

—*Matthew 11:28*

Rest. Think about that word. Realize how little you've experienced it lately.

Your labors are distracting you. The responsibilities you shoulder at work, at home, with all your relationships—they keep your mind busy with fear, anger, sadness, and turmoil.

You carry the weight of your sin with you. You drag behind you all your painful memories, broken relationships, and unhealthy behaviors.

Jesus says, "Come. Come to Me."

Take that step. Lift your eyes from your burdens and on to Him.

He waits for you to approach. With every step, the burden decreases. The weight lifts. He welcomes you into His rest. Bask in it as long as you need to today.

Take the yoke I give you. Put it on your shoulders
and learn from me. I am gentle and humble, and
you will find rest. This yoke is easy to bear, and this
burden is light.

—*Matthew 11:29–30*

Jesus invites you to take His yoke on yourself, to
join yourself with Him for a purpose: to learn
from Him.

He offers release from the weight of life's burdens and in its place the fulfillment of knowing
Him intimately. He invites you to partake of His
peace, His rest, His light.

There is a price: You are yoked, bound to
Him. But it's a bondage that is freeing because
the burdens you are used to carrying are lifted
into His care.

Have you experienced Jesus in His gentleness?
Are you enjoying His rest?

His offer stands. The yoke is waiting. He waits
to teach you about experiencing total fulfillment
as His child.

Don't you know what the Scriptures mean when they say, "Instead of offering sacrifices to me, I want you to be merciful to others"? If you knew what this means, you would not condemn these innocent disciples of mine.

—Matthew 12:7

Sacrifice is an external formality of obedience to the written law. Mercy is the natural outflow of an inner spirituality that is alive, seething with passion for God.

Many leaders in Jesus' day assumed that God wanted their lives marked by the former, which left little time and no inclination for the latter.

But Jesus reminded them that God has always desired mercy—and he quoted the prophet Hosea to prove the point.

God hasn't changed. Unfortunately, neither does a human heart unless God's grace breaks through its rigid exterior. Then the mercy can overflow through you, outward to those who need to experience it as well.

Mercy costs. But God will honor the sharing of it every time.

If you had a sheep that fell into a ditch on the Sabbath, wouldn't you lift it out? People are worth much more than sheep, and so it is right to do good on the Sabbath.

—Matthew 12:11–12

The religious leaders looked at God's written law and left out His grace. No work on the Sabbath, the law said, so no healing was permitted.

But that viewpoint made absolutely no sense to the Son of God. Anybody would rescue a sheep that had fallen into a ditch. And how much more valuable was a human being! His argument was undebatable. His conclusion was clear. His credentials were beyond reproach.

But the leaders were not convinced. Rather than see God before them in a simple yet miraculous act of mercy, they saw a dangerous lawbreaker, and they vowed to remove Him.

Jesus encourages you to do good. Don't hesitate to be merciful, even when it may not look right to others. That's what God desires.

Then Jesus told the man, "Hold out your hand."
The man did, and it became as healthy as the other
one.

—Matthew 12:13

In defiance of the rigid religious leaders, Jesus
told the man with the disabled hand to stretch it
out. And in obeying Him, the man was restored.

Simple words, a direct commandment, immediate obedience.

The man didn't look at Jesus as though His request were nonsense. He didn't question whether
Jesus really had the power. And he certainly didn't
look at the religious leaders in fear of their
reprisal.

No, he did as Jesus said, and he was made
whole. A clear example of obedience rewarded.

So why do we have such a tough time in not
second-guessing Jesus? Why have we become so
hardened to His word for us?

His word still stands. Open your ears, soften
your heart, prime yourself to respond immediately. And witness your restoration in His power.

Any kingdom where people fight each other will end up ruined. And a town or family that fights will soon destroy itself.

—Matthew 12:25

The religious leaders were accusing Jesus of casting out evil spirits by the power of Satan, which made no sense at all. But the alternative was to recognize Him as possessing the power of God Himself, and the leaders were not willing to do that.

Jesus proved the absurdity of the religious rulers' charge with these words. If He were an agent of Satan, He would in effect be destroying Satan's kingdom by freeing people from the enemy's control.

The principle He gives is worth considering. Kingdoms can be divided. Families can be divided. People can be divided within themselves.

You may be feeling some internal division today. And you end up feeling drained and defeated.

Jesus is the Reconciler. Ask Him for a spiritual victory in your life today.

If you are not on my side, you are against me. If you
don't gather in the harvest with me, you scatter it.
—*Matthew 12:30*

There is no middle ground with Jesus. He will
not accept the attitude that says, "I just don't
want to get involved."

You *are* involved in the work of God, one way
or the other. Either you're with Him, or you're
not. And if you're not, He says you're against
Him.

Apathy is destructive. Jesus tells us we're causing havoc by keeping to ourselves, scattering the
fruit that is ready to be gathered.

There's nothing wrong with taking some time
out for solitude or spiritual refreshment. But if
your goal is to escape your responsibilities as a
follower of Jesus, it could be harmful to others.

Are you with Jesus? Are you gathering with
Him? Take a step out of the safe middle ground
today. And watch what happens.

DAY 103

I tell you that any sinful thing you do or say can be forgiven. Even if you speak against the Son of Man, you can be forgiven. But if you speak against the Holy Spirit, you can never be forgiven, either in this life or in the life to come.

—Matthew 12:31–32

God is always ready to forgive every sin—even every careless word spoken against Him. He is a forgiving God.

But there comes a point when one's words reveal a stubborn, unchangeable heart. The religious leaders came to their faulty conclusion—that Satan supplied the power for Jesus' healings—as a result of willful rejection of Jesus Christ. They had abundant evidence of the truth of Jesus' claims, and they refused to acknowledge that truth.

A hardened attitude like that will have severe consequences. It can start slowly and crust over layer by layer until it's impenetrable. Ask Jesus to soften any attitudes in your life that are crusting over. His forgiveness is available to you right now.

A good tree produces only good fruit, and a bad tree produces bad fruit. You can tell what a tree is like by the fruit it produces.

—*Matthew 12:33*

Again Jesus confronts the religious leaders for attributing His miracles to Satan. Look at the fruit, Jesus says. It is good! Men and women are being healed of disease, raised from death, set free from demons.

In your mind, walk through an orchard. The soft morning sun clouds up the dew still hanging in the air. The fragrances are clean and fruity. Some trees have been struck by a blight; their fruit is small, wrinkled, brown, and much has fallen to the ground to rot. Other trees are over-whelmed with ripe fruit, glistening with the morning dew, bursting with succulence.

Look at your life today. Which tree do you identify with? Which would you like to be represented by? Perhaps your limbs are just now budding. Pray that God would bring you to full fruit, that the world around you may see and know.

Your words show what is in your hearts. Good people bring good things out of their hearts, but evil people bring evil things out of their hearts.

—Matthew 12:34–35

One's words reveal one's heart.

You know of people whose conversation overflows with encouragement, strength, and wisdom. Spending time with such people always leaves you filled with new joy and warmed by genuine love.

Other people may have a quite different effect. Their conversation focuses on themselves, the injustices they've suffered, the slights they've received. Such people can be emotionally and even physically draining. But even they can be transformed.

Your words will reveal to others what is in your heart. Spend some time in self-examination. Then keep a check on your conversation to see how you're doing. Be a blessing to others out of the abundance of your heart.

DAY 106

I promise you that on the day of judgment, everyone will have to account for every careless word they have spoken. On that day they will be told that they are either innocent or guilty because of the things they have said.

—Matthew 12:36–37

We speak with but a few movements of muscle operating tongue and lips and voice box. But our words are much more than the product of a physical phenomenon involving muscle, brain, and sound waves. They are indicators of the circumstances of the heart. And they are a witness, for or against us, in the judgment.

Words can hurt or heal. They can be careless or constructive. They can be idle or illuminating. They can share lies or love.

Observe your words today. Pay attention to the subjects you address. The tone you use. The grace you impart. That's a worthy exercise in light of Jesus' word today.

[Jonah] was in the stomach of a big fish for three days and nights, just as the Son of Man will be deep in the earth for three days and nights.

—Matthew 12:40

Some of the religious leaders wanted proof that Jesus was who He was claiming to be. After a rebuke of their faithlessness, He offered one: a preview of His destiny—the sign of Jonah.

The prophet Jonah ran from God's will only to be swallowed up by a big fish and regurgitated on the shores of the land to which God had called him. For three days and nights, Jonah could ponder God's call.

Jesus, too, would ultimately spend three days and nights in darkness. And it would prove that He had come to earth as Son of God and Savior.

This sign means Jesus knew exactly what He was facing and what the outcome would be. He knew the cross of death stood before Him, and He willingly journeyed toward it for you.

These are my mother and my brothers! Anyone who obeys my Father in heaven is my brother or sister or mother.

—Matthew 12:49–50

Jesus was talking to the multitudes when someone mentioned that His mother and brothers were waiting nearby, wanting to speak to Him. And Jesus said, "Who is my mother and who are my brothers?" (Matt. 12:48). He gestured to His followers gathered around: "These are my mother and my brothers!"

He wasn't denying or disclaiming His natural family, but He was broadening His family circle to include spiritual relationships. He indicated that whoever genuinely follows Him in the Father's will is part of His forever family. And that spiritual family is just as important as one's natural family.

How strong are the bonds in the spiritual family of which you're a part—through your church, Bible study, or fellowship group?

Do something special for one of your spiritual brothers or sisters today.

A farmer went out to scatter seed in a field. While
the farmer was scattering the seed, some of it fell
along the road and was eaten by birds.

—Matthew 13:3–4

As Jesus began to tell the story of a farmer who
flung seeds here and there, He noted that some
of the seeds fell on the trampled, hardened dirt
on the side of the road. They just lay on the
tough surface—waiting to be snatched by hungry birds.

Later, the disciples asked Jesus what He meant
by the story. And He told them that the seed was
the "message about the kingdom." When someone hears it, doesn't understand or accept it, and
just lets it lie there, the wicked one will snatch it
away (Matt. 13:19). If the soil is hardened and
trampled by the world, God's Word cannot pen-
etrate.

Today, there may be areas of your soul that are
hardened to God's truth. Prepare the soil. Loosen
it in prayer and confession. Chase the birds away,
and let God's will begin to flower.

DAY 110

Other seeds fell on thin, rocky ground and quickly started growing because the soil was not very deep. But when the sun came up, the plants were scorched and dried up, because they did not have enough roots.

—Matthew 13:5–6

The seed of God's Word, Jesus taught, can sometimes fall on rocky soil. Seed that falls in places like that flowers quickly, but it withers just as quickly because the roots cannot draw sufficient nutrients.

Jesus explains the word picture to His disciples in Matthew 13:20–21. It represents a person who hears the Word, accepts it readily, and even blooms a bit. But as soon as tribulation or persecution rises, the person bails out spiritually. Such a one hasn't sufficient depth of soul to take the heat.

Today, you may feel some rocks in your soil, some truth of God that you keep having to learn over and over again because it fades when exposed to the real world. Ask yourself what stones are hindering your growth in those areas. God can help you remove them.

APRIL 19

DAY 111

Some other seeds fell where thorn bushes grew up
and choked the plants.

—Matthew 13:7

Jesus says some seeds fall in the thorn bushes.
And while they take root and begin to grow, the
dark, tangled thorns keep them from flourishing
and ultimately choke the life out of them.

In Matthew 13:22, Jesus explains the spiritual
truth. This person hears the Word of God and is
nurtured by it until worried about "the needs of
this life and . . . fooled by the desire to get rich.
So the message gets choked out," and the person
never produces anything.

It's a strong warning to each of us not to let the
glittering lights of wealth and fame distract us.
Not to put ourselves under the burden of fear
about achieving success. Not to allow our attention to be pulled away by things that aren't eternal.

Consider with Jesus whether there are any
thorns poking at your spirit. Ask Him to remove
them before they dig too deeply.

DAY 112

But a few seeds did fall on good ground where the plants produced a hundred or sixty or thirty times as much as was scattered.

—Matthew 13:8

It is God's desire that His Word fall on good ground because the result is a healthy crop—the fruit of the Spirit. Such a person hears the Word, understands it, and allows it to produce fruit (Matt. 13:23).

Even so, Jesus acknowledges that individuals have different capacities for fruit production. And He seems to express no disappointment whether the fruit we produce is thirtyfold, sixty-fold, or a hundredfold. The fact that the seed is received and produces fruit at all is a matter of deep joy to the Lord. And it's a reminder that we needn't compare our spiritual growth with others.

Plant a seed today. Eat some fruit. And let these simple acts serve as a covenant between you and God to experience this verse yourself.

I have explained the secrets about the kingdom of heaven to you, but not to others.

—*Matthew 13:11*

Jesus' disciples were puzzled about why their Master preached in parables, which often obscured the specific point He was making. Jesus revealed to them that parables enabled His true followers to learn about the kingdom but prevented those who opposed Him from understanding.

It was the Father's will to reveal His kingdom truth to His children but to withhold it from those who had no intention of following the Son. Think of it: The God of the universe desires to entrust to His children the secrets of the kingdom.

The secret revealed here is that, with Jesus' coming, the kingdom of heaven was actually penetrating the earth.

It continues to do so today through the church and through each believer, including you.

DAY 114

Everyone who has something will be given more. But people who don't have anything will lose even what little they have.

—Matthew 13:12

Jesus reveals a spiritual principle that can encourage you to ask for more of His presence, His truth, and His will in your life. He says that those to whom spiritual truth and life have been given will receive even more, more than could be imagined or hoped for. But those who do not have them will lose whatever they have. Those blind to the Father, stubborn to the Spirit, and closed-hearted to the Son will have nothing.

Jesus promises you more than you can handle so that it overflows from your life into the lives of others around you. You may not feel today that you are experiencing that abundance. But take courage from the fact that it is promised to you and that you will experience it when you're ready. And thank Him for giving you what you have right now.

I use stories when I speak to them because when they look, they cannot see, and when they listen, they cannot hear or understand.

—*Matthew 13:13*

The religious leaders, whom Jesus called "hypocrites" and "nitpickers," followed Him to listen to Him. Not to learn from Him, but to gather evidence against Him.

They thought they saw. They assumed they heard. They pretended to understand. But Jesus knew their wicked hearts, and He purposefully taught in such a way as to keep them from fully knowing the truth because they really didn't want to know it.

Sometimes when we read Jesus' words, we think we see, hear, and understand, but we can't quite fully grasp what He's saying. But that's a different situation. He's not willfully withholding the truth from us. He yearns to share it with us when we're ready.

Keep at it. Read His Word daily. And little by little, you will see, hear, and understand.

But God has blessed you, because your eyes can see and your ears can hear! Many prophets and good people were eager to see what you see and to hear what you hear. But I tell you that they did not see or hear.

—*Matthew 13:16–17*

Perhaps more than any other people in history, those who gathered around Jesus to sit at His feet and listen to His words were blessed. They could see the Son of God, witness His miraculous power, and hear His transforming words.

We can look back on those days with envy and awe, wondering what it must have been like to be part of the multitude.

But the truth is, you are in an even more enviable position because Jesus Himself dwells within you. You have no need to be a mere participant in a huge crowd, straining to see and to hear Him from a distance. Blessed are *you*.

DAY 117

Leave the weeds alone until harvest time. Then I'll tell my workers to gather the weeds and tie them up and burn them. But I'll have them store the wheat in my barn.

—Matthew 13:30

Jesus told a story about the time to come when God will judge the people of earth. The wheat represents His children—wholesome, healthy, useful. In the harvest, they are brought safely to the barn. The weeds—the evil of the world—infect the grainfields. They will be gathered, bound, and burned.

Until that day, the two will grow together. Obviously, that only brings pain, frustration, and trouble for God's righteous ones. But Jesus promises that, in that day, "everyone who has done right will shine like the sun in their Father's kingdom" (Matt. 13:43).

It will be worth the wait. God's justice will prevail. And you will shine forever.

The kingdom of heaven is like what happens when a farmer plants a mustard seed in a field. Although it is the smallest of all seeds, it grows larger than any garden plant and becomes a tree. Birds even come and nest on its branches.

—Matthew 13:31–32

When Jesus walked the earth, the kingdom of heaven seemed a mere glint in His eye. A promise of greater things. A mustard seed–sized hope, tiny and disarmingly simple. And yet a mustard seed grows greater than any other garden plant. It flourishes into a sturdy tree, full and lush and fruitful.

In the day when the kingdom is realized fully, the contrast between what it is now and what it will be then will be even more stark than between the mustard seed and the leafy tree. It boggles the mind, but it excites the spirit because someday, that promise, that vision, that hope, will be fully realized by you.

In the meantime, the kingdom is living and active and growing. And you are part of it.

The kingdom of heaven is like what happens when a woman mixes a little yeast into three big batches of flour. Finally, all the dough rises.

—*Matthew 13:33*

Jesus tells us that the kingdom of heaven is like yeast. A bit of yeast mixed in some flour slowly permeates the whole, until it all rises.

That's the way the kingdom is designed to work on earth. God's people living, working, being in the world, permeating it. Influencing it. Affecting it. Shining in it. Until the influence spreads and builds and grows. Penetrating society, and transforming one life after another.

It's a process that will continue slowly but surely until the day when God Himself brings forth the kingdom in its totality. In the meantime, it's God's plan for His children to be at work in the world.

Wherever you go today, be like yeast. Not necessarily dramatic or overpowering, but simple and steady in the impact for God.

DAY 120

The kingdom of heaven is like what happens when
someone finds treasure hidden in a field and buries
it again. A person like that is happy and goes and
sells everything in order to buy that field.

—*Matthew 13:44*

When one truly experiences the life of the
kingdom of heaven, it possesses him. It domi-
nates her thoughts. It consumes the passions.

Jesus said it's like a hidden treasure in a field.
Once discovered, it's worth everything to possess.
In this case, a man sold everything he owned to
buy the field where the treasure lay hidden.

It's worth forsaking every material possession
to live in the kingdom. It's worth giving up every
pain and hurt that keeps us stuck in ourselves. It's
worth relinquishing every selfish dream for fame
or success or wealth.

That doesn't mean to literally sell everything
you have. That does mean to let go of it, to stop
letting your possessions and your plans and your
hopes rule your life. Let the kingdom rule instead.

The kingdom of heaven is like what happens when a shop owner is looking for fine pearls. After finding a very valuable one, the owner goes and sells everything in order to buy that pearl.

—Matthew 13:45–46

Imagine a pearl so exquisite, so valuable, that you would sell everything you owned to purchase it.

In Jesus' story, a shop owner who deals in fine pearls—who knows their value and who seeks to possess as many as he can—finds a single pearl that is worth them all.

That's like the kingdom of heaven, Jesus says. It's the most extravagant way of life imaginable. Its value is incalculable. It is beautiful beyond words. And it is worth everything.

Are those ways you would use to describe your life with God? If not, what could be keeping you from experiencing the kingdom of God in its fullness? Evaluate your walk with God. Then ask Him to lead you a little farther down the path with Him today.

The kingdom of heaven is like what happens when a net is thrown into a lake and catches all kinds of fish. When the net is full, it is dragged to the shore, and the fishermen sit down to separate the fish. They keep the good ones, but throw the bad ones away.

—Matthew 13:47–48

Imagine going fishing with the disciples on the Sea of Galilee. The nets go flying, spraying mist in the air as they're flung. Several disciples strain at the task, pulling the net back to the ship. With a hearty heave, they pull the net over the side, and a load of fish cascades to the deck.

Later, on shore, the disciples review their catch, pulling out inferior fish, unwanted creatures, and smelly trash. They are thrown away without a second thought. But then the disciples glory in their good catch of the day.

The kingdom is like that, Jesus says. God pulls in the netload of fish and separates the good from the bad. It's His business which is which. And until He makes that separation, we aren't to try to make it for Him.

Every student of the Scriptures who becomes a disciple in the kingdom of heaven is like someone who brings out new and old treasures from the storeroom.

—Matthew 13:52

Jesus notes that good students of God's Word are able to bring together both new and old knowledge—just like a homeowner who pokes around the attic and finds both new and old treasures.

God's Word had been around for hundreds of years, and most of the Jewish people knew it well during Jesus' day. Jesus had come teaching them a new way. Not a different way, necessarily, or a replacement. But a way that looked at the old with a new light.

Today, we have one Bible with the Old and New Testaments. Bible study requires constantly working old and new together. Take encouragement from Jesus' words to you today as you study the Word.

Prophets are honored by everyone, except the people of their hometown and their own family.
—*Matthew 13:57*

Jesus comes home to face doubt and questions concerning His ministry.

"Hey, who does He think He is? He's Joseph's boy—and Mary's His mother! How can He claim to do such things?" Those were the kinds of taunts He heard.

He offended the townspeople by shattering their assumptions of what people should say and do. Consequently, their lack of faith hindered Him from performing miracles in their midst. They robbed themselves of a blessing of a lifetime by their doubts and small-mindedness.

Perhaps you think you know Jesus better than you really do. And your perceptions of who He is or who He ought to be are keeping Him boxed up in your life, powerless in the face of your doubt—whether conscious or subconscious. Let Jesus be Jesus, and see what happens.

They don't have to leave. Why don't you give them something to eat?

—Matthew 14:16

Jesus was deeply saddened by the death of John the Baptist. He tried to get away, to spend some time in private grief, but the crowds followed Him. And He was filled with compassion and healed people who were sick.

As evening approached, the disciples urged Him to send the crowds home, so they could get food. But Jesus startled them with His words: "Why don't you give them something to eat?"

Can you imagine their surprise? There were thousands of people!

"We have only five small loaves of bread and two fish," they told their Master.

Jesus gave thanks and blessed the meager offering, and basketfuls of leftovers were gathered after several thousand ate.

Day after day, you ask Jesus to fix things, give you things, do things for you. Maybe today He's saying, "Why don't you do it?" He may take your risky first step, bless it, and multiply its impact.

Don't worry. I am Jesus. Don't be afraid.
—Matthew 14:27

Finally, after spending the day in ministry, feeding the multitude, Jesus sent His disciples across the sea, and He spent time alone in prayer.

The disciples had had a rough sail of it, buffeted by winds and waves. And then their Master approached them, walking on the water. They were terrified. They thought He was a ghost. He was, in fact, the Lord of creation.

But Jesus shouted these words to them, giving them courage in the midst of their fear.

Are the stormy winds blowing you right in the face, the waves of life tossing you roughly, mercilessly, relentlessly? Look, coming toward you: It's Jesus. In His power, He tells you not to worry. And He's getting into your boat with you.

Come on!

—Matthew 14:29

Fearfully the disciples stare at their Master standing on the water's surface. He has greeted them and reassured them: "I am Jesus. Don't be afraid."

Peter immediately says, "Lord, if it is really you"—notice there's still some doubt—"tell me to come to you on the water" (Matt. 14:28). "Prove it!" Peter is saying. "And by the way, that looks like fun, so make me walk on the water, too!"

Jesus says, "Come on!"

Peter's faith was strong enough to enable him to obey. And he walked toward Jesus on the water. It was Peter's idea to walk on the water, but Jesus issued the official invitation. Peter's idea may have been silly, but Jesus honored it for a reason.

He may be inviting you today to take a step out into what seems to be a silly place. Who knows? Ask Him! Then see what He says: "Come on!"

DAY 128

You surely don't have much faith. Why do you doubt?

—Matthew 14:31

Peter asked Jesus to let him walk on the water toward Him. And Jesus said, "Come on!"

Peter did indeed walk, but it turned out to be a very short one. The brisk winds frightened him. And as he lost faith, he began to sink into the sea, shouting, "Lord, save me!" Of course, Jesus did.

Peter's doubt robbed him of an experience of a lifetime. His circumstances got to him, and he looked away from Jesus.

What could happen for you if only you don't doubt? If only your circumstances don't smother your passion for life one more day?

Jesus may have gently chided Peter with these words, but they must have burned in the disciple's soul: "Why do you doubt?" Just think what could happen today if Jesus didn't have to ask you the same.

DAY 129

Why do you disobey God and follow your own teaching?

—Matthew 15:3

The strict religious leaders chided Jesus for allowing His disciples to get away with breaking the traditional teaching of the elders—the little rules that over many years grew around God's law. The disciples' sin was not washing their hands when eating bread—not for hygiene's sake but as a ritual for purification.

Jesus threw the leaders' charge right back at them and enlarged it. His disciples might have violated the tradition, but the leaders actually disobeyed God's law by focusing so minutely on the little rules that had built up on top of it.

Tradition can have a strangling effect. Some churches, and some individuals, become so tied up in "the way we've always done it" that God's Spirit has little opportunity to minister directly. Examine the traditions keeping you from growing even closer to Jesus.

All of you praise me with your words, but you never really think about me. It is useless for you to worship me, when you teach rules made up by humans.
—Matthew 15:8–9

Jesus' indictment of the Jewish religious leaders is heartbreaking. The leaders knew how to do all the right things, how to say all the right words, but their worship was meaningless because they did not teach God's way.

It makes you wonder how they reacted to His stinging charge. The truth is, their hearts were hardened against Him.

Perhaps today you're sensing a lack of meaning in what you're doing as a believer. It may simply be a spiritual dry spell. But ask yourself if your stubbornness is keeping you from genuine worship. Are you wrestling with Him to have your own way? Are you sidetracked down some meaningless doctrinal path? Spend some time today bringing your heart in line with His.

Pay attention and try to understand what I mean. The food that you put into your mouth does not make you unclean and unfit to worship God. The bad words that come out of your mouth are what make you unclean.

—Matthew 15:10–11

Jesus told the multitude this proverb, and its simple truth stung the Pharisees. Jesus knew that the religious leaders who badgered Him might have been careful about the things they put into their mouths—they were certain to wash their hands first—but that was totally insignificant in light of understanding what came out of their mouths. Their words reflected what was really in their hearts.

The point Jesus is making today is, the incidental details of your religious experience are of no importance until you deal with your heart and its spiritual condition. And the way to check that out is to watch what comes out of it.

Every plant that my Father in heaven did not plant
will be pulled up by the roots.

—Matthew 15:13

Jesus' disciples pointed out to their Master that
the religious leaders were offended by what Jesus
had said about them.

Jesus shrugged them off with this statement.
In other words, those religious leaders may look
like God's people, but they're not. They're like
silk flowers—impressive to look at but with no
life in them. And because the Father did not
plant them, they will ultimately be uprooted.

Those were the men into whose hands the religious life of the nation of Israel had been
placed. And they were frauds. Obviously, many
people recognized them as such. That's why so
many followed Jesus while He walked the earth.

But it's a good reminder for us today to be discerning in who we turn to for guidance, leadership, and instruction. Pray for a discerning spirit
because looks can be deceiving.

DAY 133

Stay away from those Pharisees! They are like blind people leading other blind people, and all of them will fall into a ditch.

—Matthew 15:14

The fate of the Pharisees lay before them. Jesus revealed His contempt for their false faith, calling them blind. As a result, those who follow them are blind. And both are destined to fall into a ditch.

Jesus certainly did not pull punches. He was honest and direct in His assessment of things as they were. Of course, He also knew the whole facts of the situation about which He proclaimed His views.

It's one thing to bad-mouth certain people. It's another to be the Judge of the universe and do so. Jesus has the authority to pronounce judgment. We don't. Not that we shouldn't be discerning and careful. But we should leave the job of judging to the One whose job it is.

If you've been offended in such a way, let go of it. Be freed from it. Give it into Jesus' hands. He knows what to do with it

DAY 134

Dear woman, you really do have a lot of faith, and you will be given what you want.

—Matthew 15:28

A woman whose daughter was severely demon-possessed approached the Savior. And He ignored her request. In fact, He didn't say a word.

She was a Canaanite, a pagan. Still, she kept after Him.

Jesus said He came to gather the lost sheep of the house of Israel, not Canaan. Still she came, worshiping Him, begging His help. Still, He wouldn't budge: "It isn't right to take food away from children and feed it to dogs." And she answered, "Lord, that's true, but even dogs get the crumbs that fall from their owner's table."

She acknowledged what Jesus was doing, and she kept asking. And He answered her with compassion.

What are we to make of this? Jesus was being honest, direct, and open to the woman's honesty and directness. And that may be the lesson you need to hear.

MAY 13

I feel sorry for these people. They have been with me for three days, and they don't have anything to eat. I don't want to send them away hungry. They might faint on their way home.

—Matthew 15:32

Jesus had spent three days ministering to the multitude, healing the sick ones, teaching the people of the ways of the kingdom of God. And still He had compassion on them.

He looked out upon the sea of faces surrounding Him, the men and women and children, young and old, wealthy and poor. And He saw in their eyes a hunger.

He had worked hard to deal with their spiritual hunger. But their physical hunger remained unsatisfied. No one asked Him to take care of their need for food. He had compassion on them.

Today, He looks at your need compassionately. He yearns to meet it for you. And He wants you to look at the multitude around you with compassionate eyes.

DAY 136

Jesus asked them how much food they had.
—*Matthew 15:34*

The disciples feel the pressure once again of feeding a multitude numbering into the thousands, all of them hungry. "Where can we find enough food?" they ask Jesus, their frustration evident. And He answers them by asking how much food they have.

Didn't they pay attention to the time Jesus fed even more people with even less to start with?

Two questions to consider today. First, are you inclined to rejoice in answered prayers, miraculous solutions, and spiritual highs and then forget them? Remembering them can increase faith day by day.

Second, how much food do you have? Do you feel inadequate to the task Jesus has set before you? Consider what Jesus did with seven loaves and a few fish. And imagine what He could do with all your resources.

If the sky is red in the evening, you say the weather will be good. But if the sky is red and gloomy in the morning, you say it is going to rain. You can tell what the weather will be like by looking at the sky. But you don't understand what is happening now.

—*Matthew 16:2–3*

The fulfillment of all the prophecies regarding the Messiah stood right in front of their noses, but the religious leaders couldn't see it. What's more, they opposed Jesus.

Somehow, Jesus didn't fit in to their interpretations. Or He threatened their power and authority over the people. Or He just scared them. So they rejected God's gift to humanity to protect themselves.

Is there an area of your faith where you have closed your eyes to what's standing right in front of you? An area in which your stubbornness is keeping you from experiencing God's perfect will for you?

Watch out! Guard against the yeast of the Pharisees and the Sadducees.

—Matthew 16:6

Just as yeast works itself into and affects a whole batch of flour, so false teachings do the same to a body of believers. And Jesus says, "Watch out!"

Watch out for the yeast of the Pharisees. That's the point of view holding that religion consists primarily of rites and ceremonies. It's a rigid legalism that teaches the way to God is in following, to the letter, a list of rules.

Watch out also for the yeast of the Sadducees. That's the point of view denying the supernatural elements of the faith, relying instead on rational thinking and materialism.

In neither view is there power for living. In neither view is God free to work as He chooses.

Watch out, Jesus says, for these views can sabotage your living, growing, vibrant relationship with God.

Don't you understand? Have you forgotten about the five thousand people and all those baskets of leftovers from just five loaves of bread? And what about the four thousand people and all those baskets of leftovers from only seven loaves of bread?

—*Matthew 16:9–10*

Jesus warned His disciples of the yeast of the Pharisees and Sadducees, and they muttered to themselves, "He's telling us that because we forgot to bring any bread with us."

But Jesus quickly corrected His slow-thinking friends. He wasn't talking about actual bread at all. Hadn't they paid any attention to the miracles of the feeding of five thousand and four thousand? How could a lack of bread be of any concern to them?

The disciples had a hard time learning spiritual lessons. And they had an even harder time understanding them.

It's easy to shake our heads at them when we read about their frustrating thickheadedness—until we realize that when we're looking at the Bible text, we're looking in a mirror.

What's Jesus trying to get you to understand today? Think about it.

But who do you say I am?

—Matthew 16:15

Jesus asked His disciples, "What do people say about the Son of Man?"

His disciples reported what they'd heard: John the Baptist, Elijah, Jeremiah, or one of the other prophets.

Then He put it directly to them: "But who do you say I am?"

Imagine their surprise at the question. After all, they were with Him constantly! They knew Him intimately. So why was He asking them a question like that?

Was He curious about their thinking? Was He testing them? Perhaps He was.

And the question still hangs in the air: "Who do you say I am?"

What do you tell others about Jesus? What does the way you live your life tell others about Jesus? The answers to these questions will answer Jesus' question today.

DAY 141

So I will call you Peter, which means "a rock." On
this rock I will build my church, and death itself will
not have any power over it.
—Matthew 16:18

Jesus asked, "Who do you say I am?" And
Simon Peter answered, "You are the Messiah, the
Son of the living God" (Matt. 16:15–16).

Jesus praised His disciple's response because he
couldn't possibly have known that answer unless
it had been revealed by the Father.

Then He adds today's word. And scholars have
debated what it really means ever since.

Don't worry about the details right now. Instead, let the force of what Jesus said hit you: As
His children, we're part of His body, the church.
It's powerful. It's forever. And it's ultimately victorious over everything that seeks to destroy it.

You are part of that unshakable rock, the
church. Nothing can break you away from it.

That truth excited Jesus. Let it excite you
today, too.

DAY 142

I will give you the keys to the kingdom of heaven, and God in heaven will allow whatever you allow on earth. But he will not allow anything that you don't allow.

—Matthew 16:19

Jesus offers His closest followers authority—the keys to the kingdom of heaven. It is the authority to forbid or permit. To prevent evil forces and to free up the spirit.

Whether we have this precise authority as His children today is not our concern. What is clear is that there is another dimension of spiritual existence. Our spirits can discern what's going on in that realm. Our prayers can make an impact in it.

But it's all under the direct authority of Jesus Christ. And we can be partakers of His authority.

Be vigilant in your prayers. Be watchful in spirit. Be bold in your requests. Don't take for granted the impact your words can make, especially when they're spoken in the power of the Lord.

Satan, get away from me! You're in my way because
you think like everyone else and not like God.

—*Matthew 16:23*

When Jesus told His disciples the fate that
awaited Him—death—Peter protested, "That
should never happen to You! You don't deserve
such a fate!"

They sound like supportive words. But Jesus
saw them for what they were: a temptation to
avoid His preordained fate.

In fact, the words He spoke to Peter—"Satan,
get away from me!"—were the same He uttered
to Satan in the wilderness (Matt. 4).

No doubt Peter was caught unawares by Jesus'
admonition. He meant only to stand by his
Friend.

But Jesus speaks the truth directly and clearly.
And what may seem to be positive is skewered as
totally opposed to the will of God.

Think about what you say before you say it.
Consider what you're saying, why you're saying
it, and who you're saying it to.

If any of you want to be my followers, you must forget about yourself. You must take up your cross and follow me.

—*Matthew 16:24*

Do you really want to follow Jesus?

Jesus tells you how to do it: Forget about yourself. Take up your cross. Follow Him.

Three steps, a few basic words. But you can spend a lifetime trying to obey them.

To forget about yourself means to put the kingdom of heaven first in your life rather than your own desires.

To take up your cross means to put to death selfish desires and be open to God's leading.

To follow Him means not only to see how He lived as recorded in the Bible but to be open and obedient to the Spirit, who will lead you moment by moment if you will listen with your heart.

If you want to save your life, you will destroy it. But if you give up your life for me, you will find it.
—*Matthew 16:25*

You may be working hard to become healthier in your relationships. To become yourself as God created you to be—not the way that it became corrupted and hurt earlier in your life.

Sometimes that process is overwhelming. We can fall prey to the fear that we'll never make it and scramble to fix the sore places with various methods.

If you're in a place like that, examine how you're trying to save your life. If Jesus is not part of the process, the process is fruitless. If you're trying everything you can, without His guidance and empowerment, to save your life, you'll end up destroying it.

On the other hand, giving up your life is the only way to find real life. And working through the process spiritually will give you the power to do that.

Give up your life for His sake. And you will find life.

What will you gain, if you own the whole world but destroy yourself? What would you give to get back your soul?

—Matthew 16:26

The world we live in is upside down. Its goals are purely materialistic, selfish, and empty. And these goals saturate the society. They taunt us, provoke us, and keep our eyes off what could bring us a truly abundant life.

We are mistaken if we think this is the real world. In the real world, the soul is the foremost possession. It is worth everything to you because it is you.

Jesus says you could have everything the world offers, but if you lose your soul, you have nothing.

The rest of the world will find that hard to believe. It doesn't fit society's perspective.

But you're not the rest of the world. You've come to realize the true value of your soul. And you want to invest it wisely. Ask God for strength today in the face of the world's counterfeit.

The Son of Man will soon come in the glory of his Father and with his angels to reward all people for what they have done.

—Matthew 16:27

Jesus gives His disciples a glorious hint of the end of time, when He will return. And He promises a reward to people who live fruitfully.

Many believers downplay the concept of rewards. It doesn't feel Christian to do good deeds with the expectation that someday, God will pay us back for them.

But it seems to be so. We don't know what the reward consists of—a pat on the back from the Savior, a celestial trophy, heavenly money, or some form of authority. Our minds probably can't conceive the reward, so we're left to guess.

Still, we can experience joy and satisfaction now when we reach out to someone in love and concern. Perhaps that's all the reward we need for now.

DAY 148

Get up and don't be afraid!
—*Matthew 17:7*

The disciples Peter, James, and John witnessed an event no humans had ever come close to witnessing. And they were terrified.

On top of a mountain, they saw the glorified Jesus. Joining Him were Moses and Elijah. And the voice of God thundered about them, "This is my own dear Son, and I am pleased with him. Listen to what he says!" (Matt. 17:5).

It's no wonder they were terrified. Imagine hearing the voice of the Father of the universe Himself! The glory about them must have shaken them to their core, exposing their humanity and neediness in the light of absolute holiness and purity. But Jesus reassured them.

God has no intention of terrifying us with His power and glory. Someday we will truly understand that.

Even now, His glory is all around you. You just may be having trouble seeing it. Today, look for it. Get up, and don't be afraid of it.

In fact, [Elijah] has already come. But the people did not recognize him and treated him just as they wanted to. They will soon make the Son of Man suffer in the same way.

—*Matthew 17:12*

Many taught that before the Messiah could come, Elijah must return.

Jesus echoed this teaching, but He revealed that Elijah had already returned. And the disciples understood that He was saying Elijah had returned in the person of John the Baptist to prepare the way for the Messiah.

But the religious leaders rejected John, refusing to acknowledge his declaration of the coming of the Lord. Ultimately, they put him to death.

Jesus told His disciples the same fate awaited Him, yet He kept going because He knew it was the Father's plan for Him. He even knew that it would provide your salvation.

You can let that realization empower you today

You people are too stubborn to have any faith! How much longer must I be with you?

—Matthew 17:17

A man came to Jesus, saying his son experienced severe epileptic seizures. He had brought his son to Jesus' disciples, but they could not cure him.

That prompted Jesus to utter today's words. They were directed to His disciples, and surely, they stung. But the words point to a heart filled with disappointment. If He didn't have hope in His followers, He wouldn't have had such an emotional response to their failure.

Jesus knew His disciples could perform mighty miracles if only they had the faith. This instance revealed their faith was still shaky. Jesus may have been disappointed in the results of their feeble attempts, but He wasn't going to give up on His followers.

He won't give up on you, either. He has faith in you.

But I can promise you this. If you had faith no larger than a mustard seed, you could tell this mountain to move from here to there. And it would. Everything would be possible for you.

—Matthew 17:20

After the disciples failed to exorcise a demon, they approached their Master to ask Him why. He answered, "Because you don't have enough faith!"

In fact, Jesus told them, if they had had faith the size of a mustard seed, they could move a mountain. Nothing would be impossible for them.

It may not be God's will for you today to move a mountain. It may be enough for you to move your feet in a certain direction, to extend your hands, to open your heart. Even these efforts require great faith at times.

Have faith today. It may not be as big as a mustard seed, but it will be a start.

The Son of Man will be handed over to people who
will kill him. But three days later he will rise to life.

—Matthew 17:22–23

Clearly this time, Jesus reveals the fate that
awaits Him. Betrayal, death, and what? On the
third day after His death, He will rise to life?

The disciples must have let that part fly over
their heads because Matthew indicates they were
"very sad."

Certainly, His death would be tragic. And the
thought of betrayal was unconscionable. And
yet, He would be raised up. There is hope.

But perhaps that last part of Jesus' prophecy
didn't fly over the disciples' heads. Maybe despite
that hopeful note, they were saddened because
they would lose from their midst their Master,
their Mentor, their Friend.

They didn't understand the indwelling ministry of the Spirit, which meant that Jesus would
still be with them. Not just *beside* them. He
would be *within* them. Just as He is within you
today.

I promise you this. If you don't change and become like this child, you will never get into the kingdom of heaven.

—Matthew 18:3

The disciples posed a question to Jesus: "Who will be the greatest in the kingdom of heaven?"

By His answer, Jesus revealed to them that they weren't asking the right question. Let's not even think about who will be the greatest in the kingdom of heaven, He's saying. Let's think about how you get into the kingdom of heaven in the first place.

Jesus says to enter the kingdom of heaven, you must be changed from the inside out. Radically transformed.

You must shrug off the adult self-importance that has choked your life and become something else entirely—a child.

Listen. Trust. Love. Play. Be simple. Innocent. Open. Spontaneous. Creative. Affectionate.

Be a child of God today, and enter His kingdom.

If you are as humble as this child, you are the greatest in the kingdom of heaven.

—*Matthew 18:4*

These words of Jesus may not have made a whole lot of sense to the disciples. They're still surprising to hear today.

After all, shouldn't the greatest in heaven be a royal personage, someone far above everyone else in terms of wisdom, or a powerful leader?

In the kingdom of heaven, the world's understanding is turned upside down. And our stereotypes of the "greatest" are shattered.

Jesus says, humble yourself, just like a child. And that will make you among the greatest in heaven.

That's a tough order for mature adults. Start today by seeing yourself crawling on to Jesus' lap, and talk to Him about it.

And when you welcome one of these children because of me, you welcome me.

—*Matthew 18:5*

Jesus lovingly pulls a child to Himself and speaks these words to His disciples. He tells them that when you open your arms and heart to a little child, you're in effect doing the same to Him.

Unfortunately, this verse tends to be overanalyzed. So avoid that temptation today, and take it at face value.

You may deal with children daily, you may volunteer to serve in a church nursery or an after-school program, or you may have few opportunities to welcome a child into your life.

Working with children is a rewarding pursuit. They can add life to you. And you can add immeasurably to their lives.

Put some skin on Jesus' words today. Reach out to welcome a child. And welcome Jesus.

DAY 156

It will be terrible for people who cause even one of my little followers to sin. Those people would be better off thrown into the deepest part of the ocean with a heavy stone tied around the neck!

—*Matthew 18:6*

Jesus says that anyone who offends a child, causes a child to fall, or encourages a child to doubt faith in Jesus will face dire consequences. It would be better for the person to be thrown into the deepest ocean, weighed down by a huge stone.

Jesus is on the children's side. So why does He allow people to abuse children? Why doesn't He strike them down before they cause the little ones to sin?

We may never understand the answer to these questions. But we do know, because Jesus tells us here, that justice will prevail ultimately.

If you must deal with childhood memories of abuse, ask Jesus for a forgiving heart and an ability to turn the memories over to Him as best as you can. Or if you know a child or an adult who is wrestling with abuse, past or present, offer your support.

If your hand or foot causes you to sin, chop it off and throw it away. You would be better off to go into life crippled or lame than to have two hands or two feet and be thrown into the fire that never goes out.

—Matthew 18:8

Is Jesus advocating self-mutilation? No. But He is drawing a distinction between life and death brought about by the way we live.

Sin is the product of the heart; Jesus has said as much. It's not the hand or the foot or the eye that actually sins; it's the heart.

Jesus is advising that it's worth doing anything you need to do to remove the temptation to sin. Because sin will lead only to degradation, depravity, and destruction.

It's better to do without some things—even your hand or foot—if they make you stumble into sin. So what's causing you to stumble? What influences are draining you of your serenity and power?

Answer these questions, and cope with the answers in God's strength.

DAY 158

Don't be cruel to any of these little ones! I promise
you that their angels are always with my Father in
heaven.

—Matthew 18:10

This comforting word from Jesus sets our
minds free to imagine what heaven must be like.

Children are to be cherished and loved. Their
angels in heaven are ever before the glory of the
Father. Interceding for them. Mediating the Father's love and protection.

Jesus has already told us that His followers are
to be as little children. That means you can place
yourself in this verse. And perhaps it's a word
your inner child needs to hear today.

The Father's glory is ever shining in heaven
with warmth and love and acceptance and grace
and protection. And your guardian angels are
ministering all that divine love to you if you will
accept it.

It feels good to be His cherished child.

DAY 159

For the Son of Man has come to save that which was lost.

—Matthew 18:11 NKJV

We are all lost, separated from God and from the life He yearns to give us. Because we are lost, our destiny is eternal alienation from God—unless He finds us. And that is why Jesus, the Son of man, came to earth: to find us.

Until we let Him find us, we remain in a lost state. And even after He finds us, we may occasionally feel lost. Cut off from true communion with Him. Estranged from some important people in our lives.

We may feel lost, but we aren't lost. We have been found. We have been saved from all that by Jesus Himself.

And that's what He wants you to know and experience today. In the midst of all your feelings of lostness, know that you are in His embrace forever.

Let me ask you this. What would you do if you had a hundred sheep and one of them wandered off? Wouldn't you leave the ninety-nine on the hillside and go look for the one that had wandered away?

—Matthew 18:12

Jesus tells a story of a shepherd concerned about a lost sheep, and in doing so, He opens our eyes to the Father's concern for His lost children. Even with a flock of a hundred sheep, one missing member is important enough to seek. And to rejoice over when found.

If God has found you, He has rejoiced over you. And that thought can bring you joy. But you may know of a sheep who is wandering away. Are you willing to follow the Father's example and search for that lost sheep? Offer yourself to talk, to sit, to pray—whatever is needed. You may soon find yourself rejoicing.

That's how it is with your Father in heaven. He
doesn't want any of these little ones to be lost.

—Matthew 18:14

God the Father is deeply concerned about His
little ones—children and those who demonstrate
a childlike faith. He does not want to lose a single one of them to eternal alienation from Him.
He wants to keep them all close to Him.

Jesus has spoken a great deal about the importance of children to the Father. His love for them
knows no bounds. It is pure, sacrificial, protective love. It is unshakable love. It is unwavering
love.

It's the kind of love He has for you. He is constantly at work to share that love in unique and
surprising ways with you.

If one of my followers sins against you, go and point out what was wrong. But do it in private, just between the two of you. If that person listens, you have won back a follower.

—Matthew 18:15

Jesus offers practical advice on settling grudges. If a fellow believer sins against you, don't keep it bottled up. Don't tell anyone else. Don't brood over the slight. Tell the person how you feel.

The person may choose to ignore you, deny your comments, or fight even harder against you. But if the person chooses to hear you, you have "won back a follower." You've reconciled. And few things on earth could be sweeter than healing a rift.

Perhaps Jesus' word today will give you the incentive you need to speak to someone. At worst, the situation won't change. But at best, you've regained a brother or sister. And that makes it worth every effort you could make.

DAY 163

I promise that when any two of you on earth agree about something you are praying for, my Father in heaven will do it for you.

—*Matthew 18:19*

Praying together can be a valuable experience. Jesus says if even two of us agree together in prayer that what we ask is God's will, the Father will do it.

That's a promise you may be taking for granted. Or worse, neglecting.

Personal prayer time alone with the Lord is crucial for your spiritual growth. But effectiveness in prayer is enhanced when you work with another believer or two.

If you're involved in praying regularly with someone else—not only for your individual needs, but for your church, your community, and your world—thank God for this promise. And try putting it into effect today.

But if you don't regularly meet with another believer to pray, today would be a good time to think about starting that discipline.

Whenever two or three of you come together in my name, I am there with you.

—Matthew 18:20

Yes, Jesus is always with you, no matter where you are.

But something unique happens when a few believers come together in His name. Somehow, Jesus is there in their midst.

Think about that. When you are with one or two others, Jesus is there with you to hear, to hold together, to answer, to guide.

He is there in the midst of your gathering to interact with you in your conversation and your prayers. That is, if your gathering is in His name. If He is invited. If He is recognized and honored.

Next time you get together with another believer or two, read this verse together. Speak to Jesus as if He were sitting right there with you, praying with you, because He is. You have His word on it.

Not just seven times, but seventy-seven times!
—Matthew 18:22

Peter asked Jesus, when a brother sins against me, how many times should I forgive him? Up to seven times?

Peter was being charitable—if not a bit proud of his humility. The traditional Jewish teaching was that an offended believer needed to forgive a brother only three times.

Jesus' answer no doubt surprised Peter. He may have even expected a word of praise for being so generous with his forgiveness. For Jesus said not just seven times but seventy-seven times. Of course, He wasn't being precise. His point was that our forgiveness should not be limited in any way.

You may have to forgive someone more than seventy-seven times before your heart is cleansed from the pain. After all, think how much Jesus has forgiven you.

The king called the first official back in and said, "You're an evil man! When you begged for mercy, I said you did not have to pay back a cent. Don't you think you should show pity to someone else, as I did to you?"

—Matthew 18:32–33

An official owed the king a huge sum: ten thousand talents. When the king ordered that the official and his family be sold to pay the debt, the official begged him to have patience. Moved with compassion, the king forgave the debt. But the official threw into prison someone who owed him money. The king heard what happened and angrily had the official tortured until his money was repaid.

God has forgiven you the ultimate debt—your very life. He paid for it with the death of His Son. So any slight you harbor bitterly in your heart is a slap in His face. He has forgiven you. He desires that you forgive others.

That is how my Father in heaven will treat you, if you don't forgive each of my followers with all your heart.

—*Matthew 18:35*

In Jesus' story, the forgiving king delivered the unforgiving official over to torturers as a consequence of his unforgiving heart.

Today's words are Jesus' bottom line to this story. And they are chilling. God the Father, whose very nature is mercy and forgiveness, despises a harsh and unforgiving heart.

That truth may frighten you today. It's really not meant to. It's intended to free you. To free you from grudges and bitterness. To free you to love and accept and forgive. To free you to be a channel of God's grace even to your enemies.

Let God liberate you of any trace of unforgiveness today. And see how much lovelier life can be when you live it God's way.

Then they are no longer two people, but one. And no one should separate a couple that God has joined together.

—Matthew 19:6

Jesus' word today makes marriage sound so simple. Two become one, joined together. Obviously, the physical meaning is evident. But what about spiritual? And emotional? And intellectual?

Is each partner supposed to lose the self in the other? Or are the partners intended to maintain their separate lives and, when convenient, come together as a couple?

Neither extreme is healthy. A marriage relationship is a new kind of thing. It's something God has put together. A man and a woman relating in a mysterious new way under His guidance.

Figuring out how it works will always be a struggle. But He is ready to give direction and support in the process. And perhaps to use you in it.

Let the children come to me, and don't try to stop them! People who are like these children belong to God's kingdom.

—Matthew 19:14

Some little children were brought to Jesus so He could touch them, hold them, encourage them, pray for them, and heal them. Perhaps protective of His time and energy, the disciples rebuked those who were bringing the children. But Jesus' priorities were higher than theirs. Ministering to children was of utmost importance to Him.

A child's trusting, open, exuberant ways illustrated for Jesus the kind of people who would enter God's kingdom. They possess a wonder about life, a joy that expects the best.

As years pass and we become more mature, that wonder and joy become increasingly stifled. And the little child within is abandoned in the past.

Hear Jesus calling to you today.

Why do you ask me about what is good? Only God is good.

—Matthew 19:17

A man asked Jesus, "Teacher, what good thing must I do to have eternal life?"

Jesus answered that no one is "good" except God Himself. And to inherit eternal life, you must come to grips with that fact.

You must accept that neither you nor anyone else can ever be good enough to inherit eternal life. And despite what the Jewish religious system had become by Jesus' day—an elaborate system of do's and don'ts that was based on but actually obscured God's law—it's a useless exercise to try to be good enough.

How hard are you trying to be good, with your own efforts, in your own strength? Come to the Teacher today, and give Him your goodness. He's willing to share His own with you.

If you want to be perfect, go sell everything you own! Give the money to the poor, and you will have riches in heaven. Then come and be my follower.

—Matthew 19:21

A wealthy young man stood before Jesus, asking Him the way into God's kingdom. Jesus told the man to obey the commandments of the law, to which the man said he had obeyed the laws since his youth. So what more must he do? he asked.

Jesus answered with these words. And the young man walked away crestfallen because he knew he could not fulfill what Jesus was asking him to do.

Jesus doesn't expect perfection of us. He is the perfect One, and He has paid our penalty for being imperfect.

Still, His heart is revealed in these words. And we should remove anything in our lives that hinders our freedom to serve Him in any way. For it is then that we will receive riches in heaven.

It's terribly hard for rich people to get into the kingdom of heaven! In fact, it's easier for a camel to go through the eye of a needle than for a rich person to get into God's kingdom.

—*Matthew 19:23–24*

Jesus and the world are at odds. The world touts a lavish lifestyle of wealth and possessions and success. Jesus shakes His head and says, "Take your choice—you can't have both."

Perhaps wealth is not an issue you feel much guilt about because you don't have much of it. If so, beware of a judgmental attitude. But also, beware of deluding yourself. Possessions seduce, and your inclination is to deny their power over you.

Look at your possessions. Look through your checkbook. Compare what you spend for the basic necessities, for the frivolities, and for charity. Ask yourself before God whether your expenditures are properly balanced. Then reread Jesus' words through different eyes.

There are some things that people cannot do, but God can do anything.

—Matthew 19:26

Jesus has just told His disciples how difficult it is for wealthy people to enter the kingdom of God. The disciples—certainly not wealthy men but generally successful in their fields—were astonished: "Who then can be saved?"

And Jesus' answer is a breath of fresh air. No one can live perfectly. You simply cannot save yourself. But "God can do anything."

He has provided a way. No matter what your circumstances, no matter what sins your past holds, no matter what problems you're wrestling with, God can do anything—even provide a way for your salvation. That's a thought to give you encouragement.

All who have given up home or brothers and sisters or father and mother or children or land for me will be given a hundred times as much. They will also have eternal life.

—Matthew 19:29

Self-sacrifice. That concept grows more foreign to our thinking by the day. Our society views having it all as a virtual right of existence. And if we don't get it, we must be free to blame somebody for our lack.

But following Jesus is a costly affair if it's to be done properly and effectively. One can't truly be a disciple and maintain an attitude of self-gratification.

There's an irony at work here. Jesus says that no matter what you must give up to follow Him, it will be restored a hundred times in heaven. And the life you will live eternally will be of glory and grandeur.

Today is a good day to accept this truth. And live in its light.

Everyone who is now first will be last, and everyone who is last will be first.

—Matthew 20:16

Jesus tells His disciples about a landowner who hired workers for his vineyard at the start of the day, in the middle of the day, and at the end of the day. At pay time, all the workers received a full day's wage. Obviously, those who had worked the whole day were upset. Why should they get the same amount as those who worked only the last hour? But the landowner pointed out that they had agreed to the amount of pay up-front. It was his right to give the workers whatever he wanted.

Jesus says, that's the way the kingdom is. God accepts anyone who chooses to come, whether early in life or on a deathbed. God is sovereign over His kingdom. His grace has opened the door wide.

You certainly will drink from my cup! But it is not for me to say who will sit at my right side and at my left. That is for my Father to say.

—*Matthew 20:23*

The mother of James and John approached Jesus and, on her knees, asked that her sons might sit on His right and left sides in the kingdom—seats of ultimate honor.

Jesus said, "You don't know what you're asking." To sit in one of the choice positions, one must suffer as He would—even to death. Yet the two men said they were willing to do that. And both men were eventually martyred.

Even so, it was out of Jesus' hands. The Father, He said, has prepared the places, and it is His pleasure to fill them.

How far are you willing to go to sit with Jesus? What are you willing to sacrifice for an eternity of communion with Him?

James and John were willing to risk it all. What would that look like in your life?

Don't act like them. If you want to be great, you must be the servant of all the others. And if you want to be first, you must be the slave of the rest.

—Matthew 20:26–27

Jesus pointed to the rulers of the Gentiles as a negative example of leadership. They lorded it over their subjects, exercising their authority with selfish relish. The arrogance of power had no place among God's people.

Rather, Jesus explained, those who are great in the kingdom are in truth those who serve others. Those who put aside selfish interests and focus on building up others. Those who forsake proud arrogance for humble, positive encouragement. Those who deny being swayed by special interests but have at heart the interests of all.

Surely, you know of faith leaders who are characterized by these traits. Draw strength from their example today.

The Son of Man did not come to be a slave master, but a slave who will give his life to rescue many people.

—Matthew 20:28

The Creator of the universe. The Authority over all. The One who possesses all wisdom and honor and power and riches. He is the Son of man.

He had every right and every ability to scrap it all—the whole earth and everything in it—and start all over. He was entitled to come in glory and power and force compliance. By rights, He should be served as the King He is.

But He put it all aside, and He came not to be served but to serve. And to give His life doing so.

That's His example. To live with no expectation of being served, but to live with every intention of serving. No matter what it took.

True servanthood is a choice, freely made, freely lived. Make it your choice.

> What do you want me to do for you?
> —*Matthew 20:32*

Two blind men sat by the side of the road, calling for Jesus as He passed by. "Lord and Son of David, have pity on us!" they called, despite protests from the multitude to leave Jesus alone. They wouldn't stop calling.

Jesus asked them, "What do you want me to do for you?"

"Lord, we want to see!" they said.

Their blindness was obvious. Jesus wanted the two men to ask for what they wanted directly. And that's a lesson in interpersonal communication you may need to hear today.

Jesus is a model of direct and honest communication. Yet He always does it with love and compassion.

Try His approach today. And prepare for some interesting reactions.

If anyone asks why you are doing that, just say, "The Lord needs them." Right away he will let you have the donkeys.

—Matthew 21:3

Jesus was preparing to enter Jerusalem. Ahead of Him, He sent two disciples to find a donkey and a colt tied together, and to bring them back to Him.

Scholars debate whether Jesus had prearranged the plan with the animals' owner or whether something more supernatural was going on. We don't know.

But we do know that when He asks something, it should be done.

Perhaps you're sensing that Jesus needs something in your life. An act of service, a sacrificial gift, an unhealthy habit given up.

Have you been mulling it over? Debating it in your mind? Thinking of the pros and cons of doing it? Weighing whether it's really in your best interests?

If you're certain it's from God, think about Jesus' words today. Then try immediate obedience.

The Scriptures say, "My house should be called a place of worship." But you have turned it into a place where robbers hide.

—Matthew 21:13

In the house of God, vendors set up shop to sell doves, exchange money, and offer all sorts of religious goods to people who came to worship God. And they did it fraudulently. The leaders were bleeding the people dry in the name of God.

So Jesus hit His limit. Righteously enraged, He careened through the temple, turning over tables, setting loose the sacrificial doves and other animals, spilling coins in every direction. His convictions were unshakable in regard to the house of God. He stood up for them. He acted on them.

The religious leaders should have known better. That's why Jesus was so angry. They were misleading God's own sheep for their own profit.

There's a time to be angry, a place to show anger, and a way to resolve anger. Let Jesus be your model for that today.

Don't you know that the Scriptures say, "Children and infants will sing praises"?

—*Matthew 21:16*

The religious leaders were indignant. Of all things, the children were crying out in the temple, praising Jesus, "Hosanna to the Son of David!" How dare they!

They confronted Jesus: "Don't you hear what those children are saying?" (Matt. 21:16). In other words, stop them! They're blaspheming! They're claiming that You're the Messiah!

Jesus answered with the words of today's verse. He validated the children's praise of Him. It was pure. Heartfelt. Honest. Free. It was perfect praise. What a contrast between the pure, wholesome praise and the bitter indignation of the so-called religious leaders.

Today is a good day to spend some time praising Jesus for who He is, just as those children did.

If you have faith and don't doubt, I promise that you can do what I did to this tree. And you will be able to do even more. You can tell this mountain to get up and jump into the sea, and it will.

—Matthew 21:21

Jesus was hungry, walking early in the morning toward the city. He saw a fig tree by the road, but it was barren. No figs, only leaves. He said, "You will never again grow any fruit!" And it immediately withered (Matt. 21:19).

The story illustrates both Jesus' humanity—His hunger, His frustration—and His deity—at His word, the tree withered.

Or *was* it His deity? Jesus declared that what caused the tree to wither was faith without any doubt. And that kind of faith, He explained to His disciples, was available to anyone.

It's a faith that can move mountains, which means it's a faith that can stand strong in the face of whatever mountains may be blocking your path to serenity and fulfillment. It's a faith that doesn't deny the mountains ahead, but deals with them in power, strength, and confidence.

DAY 184

If you have faith when you pray, you will be given whatever you ask for.

—Matthew 21:22

You'll probably pray today. You'll ask the Father to bless you and your loved ones. You'll ask Him to perform some specific acts of healing and growth and protection and provision. You've done it every day for some time now.

Some days are better than others. Some days, God seems to answer miraculously. Other days, you wonder where He is. Why He seems so silent.

Jesus asks, How much faith are you exercising when you pray? The kind of faith that moves mountains or that goes through the motions? That could be the difference between authentic prayers and mere wishful thinking.

Practice praying with faith that you will be given whatever you ask for. It could revolutionize your conversations with your Father.

When John the Baptist showed you how to do right, you would not believe him. But these evil people did believe. And even when you saw what they did, you still would not change your minds and believe.

—Matthew 21:32

John the Baptist lived a life of pure righteousness. Yet it was a life that didn't fit the format of the leaders' lives. So they didn't believe his message. What's more, they opposed him vigorously—to his death.

Some people did believe John, though. They were prostitutes and tax collectors, people who desperately needed to hear the truth about the way of freedom and deliverance and hope.

And even when the truth of John's message became obvious—verified by the miracles of Christ Himself—the religious leaders remained stubborn in their unbelief.

Some had open eyes, and they believed. Others kept their eyes tightly closed to the truth. In which group do you find yourself today?

But when they saw the man's son, they said, "Someday he will own the vineyard. Let's kill him! Then we can have it all for ourselves."

—*Matthew 21:38*

Jesus told the chief priests a story about a landowner who planted a vineyard, then leased it to some men. When the time approached to receive the fruit, he sent his servants. But the men beat and killed two groups of servants. Finally, the owner sent his son. And the men sensed their chance to claim the owner's land and run things their way. But in the end, they would receive the owner's justice.

The Owner—God Himself—had sent prophets and messengers, trying to communicate His message of love and righteousness. And failing at the hands of self-absorbed leaders. Finally, He sent His own Son, Jesus. He knew what the outcome would be—Jesus' death.

Preconceived notions can keep people blind to reality. Be careful to make sure that's not happening to you today.

The stone that the builders tossed aside is now the most important stone of all. This is something the Lord has done, and it is amazing to us.

—Matthew 21:42

The builders couldn't see the majesty of the stone they rejected. The builders were the chief priests, the Pharisees, the religious leaders of Israel. As Jesus spoke to them, He quoted from Psalm 118:22–23. And they probably still didn't get it.

The beauty of reality, to which they were blind, was that the stone they rejected would become the primary stone of God's plan. Soon, the leaders realized Jesus was talking about them. They wanted to lay hands on Him, but they decided not to because they feared the multitudes who followed Him.

You see before you the example of those who refuse to be open to the truth of God, whose hearts are calloused, whose stubbornness gets tougher. Don't let your heart grow so cold.

I tell you that God's kingdom will be taken from you and given to people who will do what he demands.
—Matthew 21:43

There would be people who listen and see and know. People who welcome God. Accept Him. Believe Him. People who, as a result, bear the fruit of righteousness and peace and joy and hope. People who freed themselves from fear, pride, arrogance, and hardened unbelief.

Jesus said to the corrupt leaders of the nation of Israel that they had their chance and lost it. God's plan would move forward with those who were humble and childlike and innocent in their faith.

Today, that is you. You are one of those people. In miraculous ways, you are doing what God demands. Count the ways. Rejoice in them. Thank God for them.

And thank God for His gift to you of being His child.

They went out on the streets and brought in everyone they could find, good and bad alike. And the
banquet room was filled with guests.

—Matthew 22:10

A king invited certain people to the wedding of
his son. He desired them to enjoy the lavish celebration. But the people didn't take his invitation
seriously. They went about their own business.
Some of them even mistreated and killed the servants who had come to invite them.

The king was furious, and he sent his armies
in judgment against those people. But still, the
wedding was to be held, and since those who had
been invited were not worthy, the king instructed the servants to invite anyone, good and
bad.

Such is the kingdom of heaven, Jesus said.

God invited His nation Israel, and they rejected Him. So He opened the party to anyone
who would come. And you're invited.

Give the Emperor what belongs to him and give God what belongs to God.

—Matthew 22:21

The religious leaders asked Jesus a no-win question: "What do You think? Is it lawful to pay taxes to the emperor or not?"

If He answered yes, the people wouldn't like it because they hated Roman rule. But if He said no, He could be reported to the Roman rulers as an insurrectionist.

Jesus saw right through their trick. And He called them on it. Then He asked for a coin: "Whose picture and name are on it?" They answered, "The Emperor's" (Matt. 22:20–21).

Then Jesus spoke today's words. Children of the kingdom have a dual responsibility. We're obligated to support the government, which is ordained by God to provide for our welfare. But above all, we're obligated to God and His kingdom.

Whatever we owe, whatever is due, and to whomever it is due, we should fulfill these responsibilities. But we're always to remember to whom our first allegiance should go.

DAY 191

And as for people being raised to life, God was speaking to you when he said, "I am the God worshiped by Abraham, Isaac, and Jacob." He is not the God of the dead, but of the living.

—Matthew 22:31–32

The Sadducees were a group of Jewish scholars who rejected a belief in the resurrection. They believed when one died, there was nothing else.

Jesus skewered their view by pointing out that God clearly stated, "I am the God worshiped by Abraham, Isaac, and Jacob." Not "I was," but "I am." And He said it long after those three men had died.

Therefore, Jesus said, "God is not the God of the dead, but of the living." Those who believe in Him always live, forever. There is no death to the spirit. And those who think otherwise are in effect already dead.

Thanking God for eternal life in heaven can give you the dose of hope and joy you may need for today.

Love the Lord your God with all your heart, soul, and mind. This is the first and most important com mandment.

—Matthew 22:37–38

Jesus boiled down all the do's and don'ts of the Pharisees by quoting this verse from Deuteronomy 6. It's the first thing God's children should do: Love Him.

With your whole heart. With all the affection and attention and emotion He deserves—which is all of it.

With your whole soul. With every fiber of your being: your personality, your gifts, your whole way of living.

With your whole mind. Intelligently, questioningly, probingly, thoughtfully.

Every cell of your existence should be aimed toward loving the One who created you and sustains you and provides for you and loves you more than you could ever approach loving Him. Center on your love for your Father God right now. Feel it; know it; live it.

The second most important commandment is like this one. And it is, "Love others as much as you love yourself."

—Matthew 22:39

Jesus summed up the entire moral code of the law with one concept: love. But He said there are two directions for that love: upward, loving God, and outward, loving your neighbors.

And in fact, there's a third direction He assumed: inward, loving yourself.

You need all three to be balanced, whole, and truly loving. You can't truly love in any one direction without truly loving in all of them.

Look at these three with your heart today. Which area seems weakest? Which seems strongest? Why do you think that is?

Which direction of love do you feel like working on today?

The Lord said to my Lord: Sit at my right side until I make your enemies into a footstool for you.
—Matthew 22:44

Jesus quoted Psalm 110 to the Pharisees to prove that the Messiah, the Son of David, is also the Son of God. For David called his son "Lord." So to call the Messiah "Son of David" doesn't really go far enough.

The ironic truth behind this, however, is that Jesus was speaking of Himself, right before them. Some understood that truth and acknowledged it. Others rejected it.

And from that day on, Matthew tells us, no one dared to question Him anymore.

Soon, Jesus would face death. And then the Resurrection. At that time, in victory, the Lord God invited Him to sit at the seat of honor and authority, at His right side.

There He now reigns. There He now prays for you and hears your prayers. There He guides and loves and blesses. Right now, He's waiting for you there.

So obey everything they teach you, but don't do as they do. After all, they say one thing and do something else.

—*Matthew 23:3*

Do what they say, not what they do." That's Jesus' advice to the people regarding following the religious leaders. And it's likely something you've heard as a child or even spoken as an adult.

The Pharisees knew the law of God inside and out. But their practice didn't reflect the true meaning and message of that law.

Jesus has summarized that law in the single word *love*.

That was not a word the Pharisees lived by. Rather, they loved to lord it over others. To enjoy their position and take advantage of it. To point out others' defects and faults and mistakes and sins.

But love? That wasn't something they did. Much to Jesus' disappointment.

Don't live that way, He says. Pay attention to the law of love. Live it freely, magnanimously, lavishly.

But none of you should be called a teacher. You have only one teacher, and all of you are like brothers and sisters.

—Matthew 23:8

The religious leaders were teachers. They knew the answers. They even knew the right questions. But assuming the title of "teacher" was a means of raising oneself over others.

Jesus says, don't do that. Don't use that title because only the Messiah—Jesus Himself—is the true Teacher.

"You are like brothers and sisters," He declares. Brothers and sisters in Christ. Together, forever. Equal in value to God. Learning from each other and from Him. That's the way He intends it to be.

Today, let Jesus be your Teacher. He's willing and able to guide you through God's Word and illuminate its truths through the Holy Spirit. Why not call some friends and ask them to join you in studying God's Word?

Don't call anyone on earth your father. All of you have the same Father in heaven.

—Matthew 23:9

There's really only one Father. God the Father. Abba. Daddy.

Yes, you have or had an earthly father. And Jesus isn't saying earthly fathers shouldn't be called fathers. He's pointing out that when it all comes down to it, your heavenly Father is most important. He is your preeminent Father.

Your heavenly Father is waiting for you with outstretched arms whenever you need Him. Always ready to take you to His bosom, listen to you, and comfort you.

There's only one Father, but He's the God of the universe who knows you intimately and loves you totally.

Let Him do that with you today.

If you put yourself above others, you will be put down. But if you humble yourself, you will be honored.

—Matthew 23:12

Build up your ego on earth, and it will be deflated later. Live a humble, sacrificial life on earth, and be exalted for all eternity.

Unfortunately, many people don't look at the long term. They get stuck in the here and now, figuring that's all they have and they'd better grab whatever they can while they can. But they only lose out in the long run.

What's more, that kind of life doesn't satisfy anyway, deep down. The joys of living a life of pure, genuine servanthood, sacrifice, compassion, and love are more valuable than any possession or flattery or power could be.

The religious leaders of Jesus' day didn't understand that. Their lives were preoccupied with position, privilege, and prestige. Learn from their negative example today.

Humble yourself. And discover the joys that last forever.

You Pharisees and teachers of the Law of Moses are in for trouble! You're nothing but showoffs. You lock people out of the kingdom of heaven. You won't go in yourselves, and you keep others from going in.

—Matthew 23:13–14

Jesus expressed deep dismay and even anger toward the religious leaders of His time. Not because they hadn't entered the kingdom of heaven—although that was sad enough. But because they hindered others from entering.

Their antagonism toward Jesus caused many people to refuse to follow Him. After all, if their religious leaders opposed Him, why should they follow Him?

That kept the kingdom of heaven shut up to many. And for that, the Pharisees and teachers would be judged.

People in your life look to you for direction. Ask yourself how you're portraying the kingdom of God to them through the attitudes you harbor, the words you speak, and the actions you live out.

You blind Pharisee! First clean the inside of a cup, and then the outside will also be clean.

—*Matthew 23:26*

The Pharisees looked good on the outside. They were scrupulously careful to observe every jot and tittle of the law regarding ceremonial cleanliness. But God desired inner cleanliness and holiness.

Jesus acknowledged their exterior cleanliness: "You wash the outside of your cups and dishes, while inside there is nothing but greed and selfishness" (Matt. 23:25).

What good is an externally clean cup, after all, if the inside is degraded and dirty? But emptying the inside—scrubbing it through repentance, being cleansed with God's forgiveness, shining with purity—makes the cup truly clean.

Look at the cup of your life today. What's in it?

Jesus desires more than anything to fill your cup with His new wine of peace, forgiveness, and grace.

You Pharisees and teachers are in for trouble! You're nothing but showoffs. You're like tombs that have been whitewashed. On the outside they are beautiful, but inside they are full of bones and filth.

—*Matthew 23:27*

In Jesus' day, cemeteries were usually caves that had been whitewashed so a person couldn't miss seeing them. Because coming in contact with a grave—even accidentally—made a person ceremonially unclean.

They were clean and dazzlingly white. In the sunlight, the sight would be stunning. And yet they held dead bodies.

That was the kind of disgusting picture Jesus painted of the hypocritical religious leaders.

You live in a world where people are attractive and clean. But inside, they're dead.

Ask God for discernment to know how to help these people and an opportunity to extend that help.

Jerusalem, Jerusalem! Your people have killed the prophets and have stoned the messengers who were sent to you. I have often wanted to gather your people, as a hen gathers her chicks under her wings. But you wouldn't let me.

—Matthew 23:37

Jesus' heart is broken over the rejection of His own people. God's people, the nation Israel, had been given a wonderful privilege of relating directly to Him. And yet, time after time, they rejected His message and His messengers.

Many people refused to hear what God would say. As Jesus ministered in their midst, the leaders continued to shut their eyes and ears to the true ways of God. And even to plot the death of God's own Son.

Still, Jesus mourns over the loss. And yet even now He yearns to gather the people of Jerusalem together, to convince them of His love and desire for their eternal happiness.

Jesus wants desperately to be your Friend, your Lord, the Lover of your soul. Climb under His wings. You are His eternal child.

Do you see these buildings? They will certainly all be torn down! Not one stone will be left in place.

—Matthew 24:2

Jesus and His disciples left the temple, walked away, then looked back at the grand buildings of the massive temple complex. Jesus must have shocked His followers with His words. See these stones? They'll just be rubble.

And His words proved true. A few decades later, the temple was destroyed, its stones pried apart, and tumbled to the ground.

Nothing made by human hands is permanent. Only God's plan is unyielding.

There may be a temple in your life. Something huge and unmoving. Something that may not be part of God's long-term plan for you.

It may look good. But it may be blocking your relationship with God. Ask God to start tearing it down today.

Don't let anyone fool you. Many will come and claim to be me. They will say that they are the Messiah, and they will fool many people.

—Matthew 24:4–5

False Christs. They would be a sign, Jesus told His disciples, of the end of time. But they can be a problem in any age.

Those who come to you proclaiming that they are of God may not necessarily be. That's one reason God indwells you in the form of the Holy Spirit—to give you discernment of other spirits. To sense whether or not someone is a genuine brother or sister. To know, deep down, whether what people say rings true with His Word.

Be open to a new way of looking at old truths. But be discerning and thoughtful, aware of subtle distinctions in meaning.

Ask for Jesus' guidance and discernment, for He is more than willing to give them to you because He wants you close to Him at all times.

You will be arrested, punished, and even killed. Because of me, you will be hated by people of all nations.

—*Matthew 24:9*

Jesus tells His closest followers that, in the end times, at the culmination of history, those who follow Him will be hated, tortured, and even killed. Just because they follow Him.

Such tribulation hasn't yet manifested itself in our midst. There are some areas of the world, however, where this verse is happening daily. And fellow brothers and sisters deserve our prayers today.

But this verse is worth pondering. Obviously, to those who are committed to Christ, that commitment is worth even their lives. They are willing to face arrest, hatred, and death for His sake.

Is your relationship with Jesus so deep, so strong, so alive that you could say the same? Imagine what you would say or do in the face of severe opposition. Would you be prepared?

Evil will spread and cause many people to stop loving others. But if you keep on being faithful right to
the end, you will be saved.

—*Matthew 24:12–13*

If you think life is difficult now, imagine living
during the end of the age.

Evil will abound. And in the face of it, many
people will stop loving God. It's a dark picture,
virtually hopeless, except for the few words Jesus
adds about the faithful.

Endurance is the hard work of faith. Keeping
after it, trudging onward, when there seems to be
no reward for the effort. But there will be. Jesus
promises it.

There will be salvation. Freedom. Release.

In the times when you feel like giving up, Jesus
says hold on. Hold on to Him. Grasp His outstretched hand. Let Him pull you along to the
goal.

When the good news about the kingdom has been preached all over the world and told to all nations, the end will come.

—*Matthew 24:14*

The message of God's love and provision for all of humanity is of foremost importance to the Father. Preaching the good news is the last thing that will happen before the end. One last chance. One final invitation. Because it's that important.

How important is it to you that you help spread that word? How often do you find yourself ministering to someone in need with the love of Christ, in deed and in word? The extent you do these things is the extent to which you have God's heart in your own.

Today, you may feel you need love and acceptance more than you can give them. If that's true, ask God to work through the stresses and strains that are toughening your heart muscles, and fill you with His love and comfort. Then ask for an opportunity to share the Bread of Life.

The coming of the Son of Man will be like lightning that can be seen from east to west.

—Matthew 24:27

Try as you might, you can't ignore lightning. It's brilliant, surprising, immediate, and spectacular. In the dark night sky, it dazzles the senses. You can't predict it. It just happens. And in an instant, it's done.

That's the way the return of Christ will be. Instantaneous. Dramatic. Spectacular. And it's only fitting, for the Son of God is all-powerful, all-present, and all-knowing.

Jesus is all-powerful. He was the agent of creation; it is in His power to do anything within the will of the Father.

Jesus is all-present. As your Savior, He is with you always.

Jesus is all-knowing. He knows what you're experiencing and how you're feeling. And He understands.

Let these truths sink deep into your heart and soul today. Then be ready for anything.

Then a sign will appear in the sky. And there will be the Son of Man. All nations on earth will weep when they see the Son of Man coming on the clouds of heaven with power and great glory.

—*Matthew 24:30*

Jesus is our Brother, our Friend. He is with us where we are, hearing us, healing us, knowing us, providing for us. But don't get stuck with that picture of Him because at the same time, He is the Lord of power and glory. And His return to earth will be like nothing ever witnessed before.

He is above all, shining with the holiness of His glory. He is to be worshiped and adored for who He is. Yet, He is always within our reach.

His coming demonstrates His power and glory. Let it prompt you to praise and worship Him with fresh vigor today.

Jesus is coming soon. But He can come to you in all His power and glory, in all His intimate love and concern, right now.

The sky and the earth won't last forever, but my words will.

—Matthew 24:35

You can count on Jesus' words. You can trust His promises to you. You can rely on the fact that they are true for you, for anyone, forever. They're even more permanent, more reliable than anything in creation, even heaven itself.

Jesus' words are health and hope and healing if you will hear them, heed them, and hold them in your consciousness.

He is speaking to you today. He is telling you what you need to hear in light of your needs, your gifts, your pains, your problems, your hopes, your dreams. He knows you inside and out. He knows what you yearn for in life. He knows what you struggle with. And He speaks to you in the midst of all that.

Hold on to His words. They are life for you. They are the answer for your questions, the hope for your doubts, the freedom for your chains.

DAY 211

No one knows the day or hour. The angels in heaven don't know. . . . Only the Father knows. . . . So be on your guard! You don't know when your Lord will come.

—*Matthew 24:36, 42*

What would happen if Jesus came back physically today?

It could happen. Who knows? Only the Father knows when that will be. Not you, not even the angels of heaven. Only the Father.

Therefore, Jesus says to be on your guard—be ready.

You don't know when it will be. You can't schedule it in. God moves as He will.

What does that mean to you? Where should your life be? How far should you have grown before He returns?

Are you ready? What would it take to be ready?

Think it through. Pray about it. Ask Him to help prepare your heart. Then think what it would be like to experience such a divine surprise today.

Servants are fortunate if their master comes and finds them doing their job. You may be sure that a servant who is always faithful will be put in charge of everything the master owns.

—Matthew 24:46–47

Faithful and wise servants are busy doing what their master instructed them to do while he was away. Then when the master returns and finds them at work, the servants will be blessed. In fact, they will be rewarded because they were found worthy.

That's the story Jesus told His followers. While He, the Master, is away, be busy doing what He has asked you to do. So when He returns, you will be rewarded eternally.

That's a reminder that can keep us going in the work of faith.

If your Master were to return today, how faithful and wise would He judge you to be? That's a standard to aim for as His child.

While the foolish girls were on their way to get some oil, the groom arrived. The girls who were ready went into the wedding, and the doors were closed.

—Matthew 25:10

Jesus is the Bridegroom. His children are the bridesmaids, responsible for preparing the bride to meet the Bridegroom at the wedding.

In the wedding procession, they were to carry lamps. At the moment the Bridegroom's arrival was announced, some of the girls were ready for the wedding. But others didn't have the oil they needed to light their lamps. They had to go and buy oil. And while they were gone, the Bridegroom arrived.

The girls whose lamps were oil-filled were ready. They entered the hall for the wedding. Those who were unprepared were left outside.

Fill your lamp with oil today. Be prepared in mind, soul, body, and spirit to come to the wedding.

"Wonderful!" his master said. "You are a good and faithful servant. I left you in charge of only a little, but now I will put you in charge of much more. Come and share in my happiness!"

—*Matthew 25:21*

Before a man traveled to a far country, he called his servants together and gave them substantial sums of money, according to their abilities. Two servants started out with different amounts, then ended up with different amounts, but both earned a 100 percent return. And both earned their lord's praise.

That's the way the kingdom of heaven is, Jesus says. The Lord has given you talents, gifts, abilities, and desires. His hope is that you use them, invest them, and reap the harvest from them. With the end result that you receive the Lord's praise. And eternal reward in the form of rulership. And eternal joy in His presence.

What are your gifts? How do you think God desires that you serve Him? Put your gifts to work for Him.

Everyone who has something will be given more, and they will have more than enough. But everything will be taken from those who don't have anything.

—*Matthew 25:29*

When Jesus told about the servants who had received talents, invested them, and earned their lord's blessing, a third servant was in the picture.

Unfortunately, he was lazy and ineffective. He was given one talent, and he buried it to make sure he could give it back.

The master was not pleased. He took the talent away from the servant, Jesus said, and gave it to the one who had earned five more.

Today's word is Jesus' summary of the story. Those who put their gifts and talents to work for the Lord will be given even more. In fact, they will have more than enough. But those who fail to live as a follower of Christ will have nothing.

The Lord will honor the faithful use of your talents and gifts.

Then the king will say to those on his right, "My father has blessed you! Come and receive the kingdom that was prepared for you before the world was created."

—Matthew 25:34

People who truly belong to Jesus Christ will receive an invitation that will surely fill the heart to exploding with love and wonder.

The kingdom is yours forever! And its glory and majesty are beyond your mortal understanding. It has been waiting for you since the world itself was formed. And in the waiting, it has become even more glorious.

What have you done to deserve this? Nothing.

God's boundless grace and love for His children alone can account for this magnanimous gift. He holds it out to you now. Someday, you will actually enter in and experience it yourself. But in the meantime, revel in the promise. Anticipate the blessing. Imagine the inheritance that awaits you.

When I was hungry, you gave me something to eat, and when I was thirsty, you gave me something to drink. When I was a stranger, you welcomed me, and when I was naked, you gave me clothes to wear. When I was sick, you took care of me, and when I was in jail, you visited me.

—Matthew 25:35–36

Jesus is saying *He* is hungry, thirsty, a stranger, naked, sick, a prisoner. And when we reach out to people in desperate need, we are reaching out to Him.

There are many hurting people around you. They may be physically ill, or they may be dealing with life-threatening losses of food and shelter.

Today, look for an outlet for your ministry for Jesus. And to Jesus. If you need suggestions, call your church or community center.

And as you do, remember Jesus' words: "Whenever you did it for any of my people, no matter how unimportant they seemed, you did it for me" (Matt. 25:40).

You will always have the poor with you, but you will not always have me.

—Matthew 26:11

A woman came to Jesus, carrying a flask of expensive fragrant oil. She poured it on His head as an act of humble service and care for Him.

His disciples couldn't believe what they were seeing. "Why this waste?" they muttered. That oil could have been sold and the money given to the poor.

That was certainly a commendable idea. And very Christian. But Jesus rebuked them.

Jesus isn't minimizing the plight of people who are poor. He is saying that when a unique opportunity to serve comes along, take advantage of it.

You'll always have opportunities to serve people who are poor because they'll always be around, and they should be served. But be aware of the one-of-a-kind, once-in-a-lifetime opportunities that may never pass your way again. The woman was, and her humble act will never be forgotten.

DAY 219

Take this and eat it. This is my body.
—*Matthew 26:26*

Jesus and His closest friends gathered in an upper room of a home in Jerusalem for a final meal together. The events that lay before the Lord haunted their gathering.

They observed the Passover meal together. The sacrifice of the lamb was recalled, salvation from the angel of death.

And Jesus took the bread that was part of their meal, blessed it, and broke it. Then He gave it to His disciples. And perhaps He startled them with the words of today's verse.

The Bread of Life. The body, about to be broken for all, is foreshadowed in the broken unleavened bread. The sacrifice of His life on the cross the next day is appropriated by each of us when we remember and eat the bread of Communion. And in a very real way, by eating the bread, we bring Him and His work into our lives anew.

Take this and drink it. This is my blood, and with it God makes his agreement with you. It will be poured out, so that many people will have their sins forgiven.

—Matthew 26:27–28

In the last meal with His followers, Jesus offered bread and a cup of wine. He thanked the Father for it, fully realizing what it represented: His own blood. And He spoke the words you've just read.

The blood would inaugurate a new covenant, a new agreement between God and humanity. A covenant of grace, mercy, freedom, and acceptance. A covenant guaranteed by the blood that Jesus Himself would shed, cleansing blood that removes the stain of sin, and its power, from our lives. A covenant that stands forever, ensuring our full acceptance by the Father because of what His Son has accomplished for us.

Drink it in. Experience it. Understand it. Accept it. And thank Him for it.

DAY 221

From now on I am not going to drink any wine, until I drink new wine with you in my Father's kingdom.

—Matthew 26:29

The occasion was somber. Jesus' disciples knew they were saying good-bye to their Master, their Friend. The next day He would face death. He would be removed from their midst. His words, His laughter, and His presence would be gone.

He shared with them the bread and the wine as a memorial to His work, as a means through which He would continually minister to their souls and provide them—and all believers—with spiritual sustenance.

But there is a hope to look forward to. There will be a day when Jesus drinks new wine, when the kingdom is inaugurated for eternity. The memorial supper is a dim preview of the marriage feast of the Bridegroom and His bride.

Today, ask God for a foretaste of that banquet, spiritually and emotionally. And let it restore your hope for the real thing.

I am so sad that I feel as if I am dying. Stay here and keep awake with me.

—Matthew 26:38

Jesus knew full well the agony He faced. Not the death He would suffer on the cross itself, but the fact that He would be made sin on our behalf—a situation that must have been virtually impossible for Him to conceive in His divine holiness.

In His humanity, He was so sad it was killing Him.

Jesus asked His closest friends to stay with Him. To support Him with their presence. He needed human companionship in His darkest hour. And He asked for it directly.

Many times when we feel our lowest, when we need the supportive touch of another, those times are the hardest to ask for what we need.

When you get in that place, follow Jesus' example. Ask for what you need. And if you have trouble finding someone to be there with you, remember that Jesus is always waiting.

My Father, if it is possible, don't make me suffer by making me drink from this cup. But do what you want, and not what I want.

—Matthew 26:39

In His agonizing last night in the Garden of Gethsemane, Jesus threw Himself down before His Father in prayer, begging Him to remove the immense burden of death for our sin that awaited Him.

It went against everything that Jesus was—the sinless Creator, the Son of the living God, the all-powerful Lord. He faced the devastating prospect of also being the sacrificial Lamb, the One who became sin for us.

Yet, despite its horror, Jesus was willing to do what He needed to do. He yielded His feelings for the will of His loving Father. The sacrifice of His body was preceded by the sacrifice of His will.

We are to yield our souls and our spirits to the Father's guiding hand that we, too, might be responsive to His will—whatever it may be.

DAY 224

Can't any of you stay awake with me for just one hour?

—*Matthew 26:40*

Jesus was in the midst of the struggle of His life, and He had turned to three of His disciples for support and comfort, asking them to be there with Him, to watch and pray. But they fell asleep.

It wasn't much to ask of friends. And yet they failed. It was late and dark, and they were sleepy. You know the feeling.

Imagine Jesus' disappointment. Sure, He understood the reasons. But in the face of deadly fear, He really needed support.

Maybe there's someone in your life who has asked for your support, and you've yet to take the request seriously.

Be aware of such opportunities today. Don't let yourself get sidetracked when a friend needs support. It's a high calling. And it can work both ways.

Stay awake and pray that you will not be tested. You want to do what is right, but you are weak.

—*Matthew 26:41*

Jesus calls for alertness. Aliveness. Awakeness.

Stay awake and pray. Keep in contact with your Father. Because if you don't, it's easy to slide into behaviors and attitudes that can be unhealthy.

It's the continual battle of your spirit and your flesh. Your spirit—the lively, deep part of you that God touches and energizes—is always willing to obey. But the flesh—the body with its lusts and laziness—can pull you down. It needs the energizing power of your spirit to get it moving. And that won't happen naturally. It takes a lively realization to stay awake and aware.

That's what Jesus asked of His disciples. It was a struggle for them. They failed. They fell asleep.

Wake up. Watch. Pray. Continually.

DAY 226

But all this happened, so that what the prophets wrote would come true.

—Matthew 26:56

Time after time, event after event during the final days of His life on earth, Jesus pointed to the Old Testament prophecies concerning the Messiah.

He knew ahead of time what would happen because He knew the Word.

And everything the prophets foretold concerning the Messiah occurred with Jesus Christ. In fact, Jesus said, "All this happened, so that what the prophets wrote would come true."

Today, this means you can trust what you read in the Bible.

The prophets were God's messengers, bringing His Word to His people. What they said as recorded in the Old Testament has either already occurred or will occur.

You can trust them because they spoke the Word of God. That doesn't necessarily mean you'll always understand what they wrote. But take comfort that you can trust them because you trust God.

I tell all of you, "Soon you will see the Son of Man sitting at the right side of God All-Powerful and coming on the clouds of heaven."

—*Matthew 26:64*

The situation is grim for Jesus. He faces the religious council called the Sanhedrin; He is forced to answer their charges.

The high priest charges Him, "Tell us if You are the Christ, the Son of God!" And Jesus answers, "It is as you said" (Matt. 26:63–64 NKJV).

Jesus acknowledges His deity. He is indeed God the Son. And then He offers a vision of Himself in the future. Sitting in the seat of authority and power and rulership. Coming on the clouds of heaven in returning to earth.

It's a glorious image. A wonderful hope. A loving testimony.

And the high priest rips his clothes: "He has spoken blasphemy!" (Matt. 26:65 NKJV). His blindness to the truth is pathetic. And yet it is all part of the plan.

Take comfort in Jesus' clear words about who He is and what He shall do because you're His child and you're part of it all.

"Eli, Eli, lema sabachthani?" which means, "My God, my God, why have you deserted me?"
—*Matthew 27:46*

Naked. Bleeding. Bruised. Crushed. Hanging by His skin and bones on a rough wooden cross.

Darkness has fallen over the land. A chilling darkness of the soul.

People huddle around Him, either to curse Him or to mourn for Him.

And with a loud voice, He cries out to Father God. His Daddy has forsaken Him. Abandoned Him. Left Him completely out in the cold. Physically, emotionally, spiritually. Why? *Why?*

The pain of the spikes through His wrists and ankles is nothing compared to the pain of His broken heart.

It was your pain He carried that day. Your cry on His lips. Let Him carry your pain of abandonment right now. After all, He has already died for it.

Rejoice!

—Matthew 28:9 NKJV

The women who went to Jesus' tomb to care for His hurriedly buried body experienced something no human could have been prepared for. An earthquake, a brilliant angel descending from heaven to roll the stone away, a revelation of an empty tomb. And a word of comfort: "Don't be afraid."

They were sent on their way to tell the disciples that the Lord Jesus lived and walked. And on their way, breathless and reckless with joy and amazement, they met Jesus. "Rejoice!" He said.

They fell to the ground in worship, grabbing on to His feet.

And He, too, told them, "Don't be afraid." He had escaped from death. He lived anew. Rejoice! That's all the women could do.

Everything else faded away. All that was left was a risen Savior. And that was enough.

He is still risen today. And He invites you to rejoice, too.

I have been given all authority in heaven and on earth!

—Matthew 28:18

Just before He departed from earth in His resurrection body, Jesus met with His closest friends. They had been with Him during astonishing days after His death, witnessing strange sights and seeing their Lord in a new light. And He was giving them a final word.

In so doing, He revealed that His words had the full force and authority of the God of the universe behind them because the Father had given Him all authority over heaven and earth.

Yes, there are times in your life when it seems that no one is in control, even Jesus. Times of loneliness, chaos, weakness, pain. But these are the very times to turn to the One who is in authority over you and your world because He has the power to act in the will of the Father.

Go to the people of all nations and make them my disciples. Baptize them in the name of the Father, the Son, and the Holy Spirit, and teach them to do everything I have told you.

—*Matthew 28:19–20*

G o," Jesus says. Move. Take action.

"Make disciples." Don't keep Him a secret from anyone. He is the Savior of all. Live the life of a child of God in their midst, so people will become His followers, His students, His friends.

"Baptize them." Bring them into the family. Introduce them to the triune God and the role each person of the Godhead can play in their lives.

"Teach them." Pass on His truth. Share His Word and the comfort and challenge it can bring.

It's quite an assignment. But it can become the natural outflow of your life because when Jesus becomes the focal point of your life, His light will radiate from it.

Ready? Go.

I will be with you always, even until the end of the world.

—*Matthew 28:20*

The last words of Jesus that Matthew records in his gospel assure us that Jesus is always present with us. In our midst. In our hearts and lives. In our pain and problems. In our fears and frustrations. In our loneliness and laziness.

Too often we become so distracted by the circumstances of our lives that we fail to remember there is One with us who is in authority over heaven and earth. And who can use the circumstances for our good.

No matter what we do, no matter what happens to us, He will always, always be with us.

He will never leave us or turn His back on us. We are His beloved children. He yearns to see us grow stronger in His love and in our spirits.

And if you'll let Him, He will be working with you toward that end, even to the end of the world.

DAY 233

The time has come! God's kingdom will soon be here. Turn back to God and believe the good news!
—*Mark 1:15*

Jesus, the Son of God, came to earth.

And in doing so, He ripped through the fabric of time and space, bringing the divine, the eternal, the all-powerful One into the world of the created.

The One who was the agent of creation came to breathe the air, drink the water, and interact with men, women, and children. God in human form laughed, wept, whispered, and shouted. He was one of us.

But it didn't happen until the time was ready, the plan of the triune God was ready to play itself out. And by coming to earth, Jesus brought the kingdom closer to all of us.

A response is called for in all this: "Turn back to God and believe." Two sides of one coin: Turn from your evil, selfish ways, and trust in God's ways.

It's the gospel, the good news. And it's for you today.

DAY 234

Be quiet and come out of the man!
—*Mark 1:25*

A man possessed by an evil spirit confronted Jesus as He walked through Capernaum. The spirit immediately knew who He was: "Jesus from Nazareth, what do you want with us? Have you come to destroy us? I know who you are! You are God's Holy One" (Mark 1:24).

Jesus had no patience with the evil spirit: "Be quiet"—literally, be muzzled—"and come out of the man!"

The evil spirit must obey the Lord, "God's Holy One." And it did.

The people, understandably, were amazed: "It must be some new kind of powerful teaching! Even the evil spirits obey him" (Mark 1:27).

It was new. No one had ever demonstrated such authority over evil spirits.

The evil spirits recognized who He was. But Jesus faced three years of doubt and opposition from people.

Today, recognize His authority over all things, both the good and the evil. And be amazed.

DAY 235

We must go to the nearby towns, so that I can tell the good news to those people. This is why I have come.

—*Mark 1:38*

The disciples were exhausted by a long, hard night with Jesus, who healed many people. And when they arose the next morning, they couldn't find their Master.

Jesus had gotten up early to get some needed spiritual nourishment, to talk with His Daddy in a quiet place alone.

By the time Simon Peter and the others found Him, He was ready to go to nearby towns to spread the good news.

"Why not take some time off?" the disciples may have asked.

"This is why I have come," Jesus answered.

He knew His purpose. He knew what He was supposed to be doing. He knew what He needed to do to accomplish it. And that's exactly what He did.

How closely are you following that example today?

DAY 236

Don't tell anyone about this. Just go and show the priest that you are well. Then take a gift to the temple as Moses commanded, and everyone will know that you have been healed.

—Mark 1:44

A man with leprosy approached Jesus, saying, "You have the power to make me well, if only you wanted to."

Jesus wanted to. And immediately, the man was cleansed from his disease.

Jesus told him to tell no one, but to offer the sacrifices as Moses commanded. By so doing the man was validating his healing. But more than that, by presenting himself to the priest, the man would demonstrate that his Healer, Jesus, possessed the power of God, since the Jews believed only God could cure that dread disease.

Jesus said, "Just go." Even though something amazing and mind-boggling had occurred, go your way and do what you should be doing.

What could that mean in light of your life situation?

The friends of a bridegroom don't go without eating while he is still with them. But the time will come when he will be taken from them. Then they will go without eating.

—*Mark 2:19–20*

Jesus is the Bridegroom. His disciples, His followers, are His friends who are invited to the party.

A wedding in the Jewish community is a gala event, often lasting a week or even longer. Music, dancing, and joy abound. And the last thing guests would feel like doing at such a wedding is fast.

Some people didn't understand that mind-set, particularly in light of the way John's disciples lived. They focused on repentance, and going without food was part of that sober-minded process.

Jesus said that the fasting, the downside, would come later. He wanted His followers to enjoy His presence while they could.

Now, Jesus is risen. He is here. So let the celebration begin!

Haven't you read what David did when he and his
followers were hungry and in need? It was during
the time of Abiathar the high priest. David went
into the house of God and ate the sacred loaves of
bread that only priests are allowed to eat. He also
gave some to his followers.

—Mark 2:25–26

The religious leaders caught Jesus and His disciples doing something they shouldn't have, according to their strict interpretation of the law:
They were picking some wheat on the Sabbath as
they walked through a field.

Jesus answered the charge by saying, in effect,
"You think this is bad? Look at what David and
his followers did." The story He related pointed
out the blindness of many religious leaders in at-
tempting to follow God's Word to the letter
while neglecting real need.

Don't let yourself get tied up in the "shoulds"
and "oughts" when human need is involved.

Do let God's heart inform your heart. God's
heart is tuned to meet needs.

People were not made for the good of the Sabbath. The Sabbath was made for the good of the people. So the Son of Man is Lord over the Sabbath.

—Mark 2:27–28

Jesus said the Sabbath was ordained by God for the good of people—and not the other way around. They were quite within their rights to take care of their needs, to do good, to save life, even on the Sabbath.

The Sabbath was designed by God as a day of rest. A time set aside to slow down from everyday activities and focus on Him and His goodness to us during the week.

Christians today generally observe Sunday as a special day to take time off from the routine, gather for fellowship and spiritual food, and rest or enjoy leisure activities to be refreshed and rejuvenated, spiritually and physically.

Are you giving yourself time to rest the way God intended? Listen to the Lord over the Sabbath today.

Jesus told the man to stand up. . . . "Stretch out your hand."

—Mark 3:3, 5

Jesus was in the synagogue on the Sabbath. He saw a man with a disabled hand, wanting to be healed from his condition.

In healing the man, Jesus had him stand up in front of everyone in the synagogue. And then He told him to stretch out his hand.

Having the man stand up and hold out his hand would make the miracle apparent to everyone who witnessed it. But it also forced the man to take a step on his own behalf. To do something positive toward healing. To exercise his faith by taking action.

That's a lesson you can hold on to today.

Sometimes we sit back and expect God's blessings to fall on us. We seek healing from past hurts, answers to prayer like bolts of lightning. But sometimes God wants us to take the first step. And then watch Him work on our behalf.

On the Sabbath should we do good deeds or evil deeds? Should we save someone's life or destroy it?

—*Mark 3:4*

Would Jesus take the risk and heal the man with the disabled hand—and thereby work on the Sabbath?

We already know Jesus' attitude toward the Sabbath and why God created it. And we can be certain He knew that the religious leaders were watching Him, hoping to catch Him doing something "illegal."

Jesus asked a rhetorical question, equating following the letter of the law in this case with evil and destruction. He was in their presence to do good, to save life.

Jesus was healing; the religious leaders were plotting to kill. The contrast is painfully obvious.

It's the difference between having an open mind and obedient heart for God's will and getting tangled up in the minutiae of "what's right."

A family that fights won't last long.
—Mark 3:25

Jesus obviously possessed power to heal. And to hold on to their position of strength, the religious leaders attributed that power to Satan.

That didn't make sense, Jesus pointed out. If He was empowered by Satan, why would He cast out demons? That would be like having a fight within a family—and the family would eventually disintegrate.

Many families are divided in their purposes and goals. And a similar division can occur in individual lives. A lack of commitment, one way or the other, leads to divided loyalties. Nothing of importance can happen because the energy is dissipated by the division.

What are your purposes and goals for today, for this year, for your life? Are they in conflict with each other?

DAY 243

How can anyone break into the house of a strong man and steal his things, unless he first ties up the strong man? Then he can take everything.

—Mark 3:27

Satan is like a strong man. His house is the realm of sin and degradation. His possessions are the men and women who have come to live there, some even against their wills.

But Jesus has been entering that house. Only He has the power and the authority to bind the strong man, proving His superiority over Satan. And only He can plunder Satan's possessions—releasing the victims Satan has kept enslaved.

Jesus is empowered by the Holy Spirit. The same Holy Spirit that is at work in your life today.

Consider the people in your life. Have any fallen into the grip of the strong man? Pray for them to be released from Satan's clutches. And trust the One who is all-powerful.

I promise you that any of the sinful things you say or do can be forgiven, no matter how terrible those things are.

—Mark 3:28

The verse following this one highlights an exception to the rule Jesus speaks here. But He was speaking to the religious leaders who had attributed His power to Satan and thereby blasphemed the Holy Spirit—who in truth was the source of Jesus' power.

We tend to get sidetracked by that exception, tripped up by it. And we forget what Jesus said here: God will graciously forgive all sins.

Let that truth sink into your soul for a few moments. It's the promise of new life, of fresh beginnings, of freedom and cleansing. It's yours for the asking.

Have you asked for forgiveness from God, yet not forgiven yourself? Perhaps today would be a good day to make an appointment with a pastor or counselor to talk about how to experience real freedom with a renewed attitude of forgiveness.

Listen!

—Mark 4:3

Jesus began to teach by the lake. The crowd grew, becoming so large that He had to climb into a boat and go out on the water to be seen and heard.

The people jammed the shore, waiting to hear what He would say. No doubt the people were moving, trying to get comfortable, talking to one another, wondering what He would say and do.

"Listen!" He shouted. He got their attention. And then He began to tell a story.

"Listen!" Jesus says to you today. Are you waiting to hear from Him? Are you wondering what He'll tell you? Or are you preoccupied with your activities? Going about your affairs, or getting overly comfortable with the way things are?

Perhaps He's whispering, "Listen," to you right now. Or shouting it to get your attention. Listen.

I have explained the secrets about God's kingdom to you, but for others I can use only stories.

—Mark 4:11

There were many secrets about the kingdom of God. But Jesus was teaching, revealing the truth, shedding light on this divine mystery.

He proclaimed the truths regarding the kingdom of God to everyone who heard. But He taught in parables, or stories, so that only those who had faith truly understood the truth He was revealing.

What a blessing you have been invited to share in—the revelation of the kingdom of God!

It's a gift God has given you as His child. To know the greatest secret humanity has ever pondered. And not only to know it intellectually but to know it personally through Jesus.

Perhaps today, God would have you shed a little kingdom light for someone else. Share the secrets.

If you don't understand this story, you won't understand any others.

—*Mark 4:13*

Jesus had told the disciples the story of the various soils and the seed of the Word. Afterward, when they gathered with Him alone, His disciples asked about the parable. And Jesus explained that He told parables to teach the truth to the faithful, yet to hide it from those outside the kingdom. Then He chided them with the words of today's verse.

Perhaps there was laughter all around because Jesus proceeded to explain in detail the meaning of His story. His goal is that His children know and understand the ways of God.

We have the Bible, sound commentaries and other study aids, and our pastors to offer guidance to us. What's more, we have the indwelling Holy Spirit to illumine our understanding. Why not give Him the opportunity?

DAY 248

The seeds that fell on good ground are the people who hear and welcome the message. They produce thirty or sixty or even a hundred times as much as was planted.

—*Mark 4:20*

There are lots of different kinds of people. Some cold and hard as packed ground. Some unable to overcome the overwhelming rocks of life. Some overgrown with worldly weeds.

And some open and receptive to the truth. Good, rich ground. These are the genuine disciples of Jesus, and out of their lives will be created a harvest of varying amounts, depending on opportunities, gifts, and abilities.

Such souls hear the Word of God, accept it, and put it to work. They learn it and live it. And as a result, their lives are fruitful and fragrant and fertile.

That's the kind of disciple you want to be, isn't it? It all starts in your heart.

Is yours open? Ready to hear and believe and act? Loosen your soil with some time in prayer right now.

SEPTEMBER 4

DAY 249

You don't light a lamp and put it under a clay pot or under a bed. Don't you put a lamp on a lampstand?
—Mark 4:21

The purpose of a lamp is to shed light. To brighten. To clarify. To reveal.

To accomplish its purpose, it must be free and unhindered. Putting it under a clay pot or bed makes no sense. What's the point of doing that? Instead, Jesus says, it should be placed on a lampstand so that it can shine openly.

In the same way, Jesus is the Light of the World. He said so Himself. He came to do what light does.

And Jesus is part of your life today. He wants to shine through you to the world around you.

Is He able to do that? Is something dimming the light in your life? Fear? Uncertainty? Laziness? Busyness?

What do you need to do to let your light shine freely today?

SEPTEMBER 5

Listen carefully to what you hear! The way you treat others will be the way you will be treated.

—*Mark 4:24*

Jesus' word encourages you to listen. Hear. Heed. Because the more you hear Him, and the more receptive you are to His Word, the more you'll receive from Him.

If you've got your spiritual earplugs in, you can't hear. So, sooner or later, you won't have the opportunity to do so.

But if you're hungry for the truth, open and yielded to His words, He will honor that. How hungry are you? How thirsty? How deeply do you desire to know His truth?

The more you want to hear, the more you'll be able to hear. And the more you do that, the greater your capacity will be to receive the truth. And act on it.

Check your ears for plugs, your eyes for blinders, your mind for closed doors, your heart for walls. Then realize how exciting it would be to see this promise fulfilled in your life today.

DAY 251

It is the ground that makes the seeds sprout and grow into plants that produce grain.

—Mark 4:28

This word picture of the kingdom of God demonstrates the responsibility each of us has to spread the seed of the Word.

The kingdom, Jesus says, is like a sower who scatters seeds in the field. Then the sower leaves them. Plants take root and grow, and before long it's time for the harvest. But none of that is the sower's doing.

In the same way, it may be God's plan for us to scatter seeds, but it's not our responsibility to cause them to grow to fruition. Nor, when it happens, should we get any credit. It's God's doing.

You sow the message of God's kingdom; God produces the results. Neither the credit nor the blame for what happens is rightfully yours.

Even so, it all starts with some sowing. Looks like a good day to scatter some seeds, doesn't it?

SEPTEMBER 7

DAY 252

What is God's kingdom like? What story can I use to explain it?

—Mark 4:30

Jesus told many beloved parables. And all given for one reason: to give each of us a better understanding of how God's kingdom works.

Jesus would tell story after story, each looking at the truth from a slightly different angle, a different perspective. Some of them easy to grasp, others rather challenging. But all of them designed to shed light on the truth.

It's obviously very important to Jesus that we grasp how the kingdom works because by understanding it more fully, we can live it more fully.

And that's why He came. To encourage us to enter His kingdom, and then to venture out from it and invite others to join us.

Celebrate the creative mind of Christ today. He kept thinking of new ways to picture old truths. You can follow His example, too.

DAY 253

Morning has come. And Jesus has a plan. A new place to go. Different people to minister to.

As it turns out, part of His plan was the journey itself and what it would teach the disciples about faith. The decision had been made, and it would be carried out.

So why do we get so bogged down in our decision-making process? Where to go with our lives. What ministry to become involved in. What career to pursue. What person to marry. On and on the decisions come, tripping us up, weighing us down.

Obviously, Jesus had the advantage of being the Son of God, the all-knowing One. But the Holy Spirit is with us.

Today, may you catch a glimpse of His clarity and direction in an area of your life that's been troubling you. Perhaps it's a good day to make a decision.

SEPTEMBER 9

DAY 254

Peace, be still!

—Mark 4:39 NKJV

The boat is being tossed by the wind and waves, filling with water, out of control. The disciples are at the mercy of the elements. And they're frightened out of their wits. They awaken their Master abruptly, angry that He seems not to care about their fate. And all Jesus has to do is shout the order for quiet.

Wouldn't it be nice if we could wake Jesus up and He could quiet an unruly storm in our lives?

The truth is, Jesus isn't sleeping. He's not unaware. But maybe He's waiting for you to ask for what you need. To stop trying to fix it yourself. To realize you're powerless over it, but He is all-powerful.

His peace is waiting for you today.

SEPTEMBER 10

DAY 255

Why were you afraid? Don't you have any faith?
—Mark 4:40

Sometimes it seems that the disciples' lack of faith did not compute to Jesus. Of course, to the disciples, Jesus' frustration was incomprehensible. After all, they had just survived a terrifying storm by the skin of their clenched teeth.

Faith? At a time like that? It's enough that they had the presence of mind to wake their Master, so He could calm the storm for them.

And yet, Jesus' surprise at their fear and faithlessness indicated that they—human beings though they were—could have done the same thing He did.

Does anyone really have faith like that?

Have you ever experienced a deep degree of faith that changed your circumstances so dramatically that there was no doubt about its effect?

Take courage. Know Jesus is with you. But use the opportunity to stretch your faith a bit more today.

SEPTEMBER 11

Come out of the man, unclean spirit!
—*Mark 5:8 NKJV*

The man was entirely out of control. He lived among the tombs and therefore was marked by perpetual uncleanness. Night and day he wailed and screamed, mutilating himself with sharp rocks. He could not be tamed. He was possessed by an evil spirit.

And one day, Jesus came into his midst: "When the man saw Jesus in the distance, he ran up to him and kneeled down." And the evil spirit cried out, "Jesus, Son of God in heaven, what do you want with me? Promise me in God's name that you won't torture me!" (Mark 5:6–7).

Apparently, it took some time and some doing. But the evil spirit was ultimately forced to obey the Son of God and leave the man.

There may be a part of your life that feels untamable, out of control. But nothing is beyond Jesus' power.

DAY 257

What is your name?

—Mark 5:9

Jesus spoke directly to the evil spirit that dwelled within the man. And in asking its name, He forced it to reveal that many evil spirits inhabited the poor man.

But Jesus had total authority in the situation. The evil spirits knew who He was. They begged Him to send them into a herd of pigs feeding nearby. He did, and the herd ran into the water and drowned.

The event so frightened witnesses that they fled. But when they returned, they found the man who had been demon-possessed "in his right mind" (Mark 5:15).

Fear not. Jesus has absolute authority over what is seen and unseen. And if the seen in your life is chaotic today, imagine what must be going on unseen.

He is able, and He is willing, to rule over the chaos of your life. Don't fear that; welcome it.

SEPTEMBER 13

Go home to your family and tell them how much the Lord has done for you and how good he has been to you.

—Mark 5:19

The man who had been demon-possessed had experienced total cleansing and revitalization at the hand of Jesus. He was a new man. And though the townspeople feared Jesus and begged Him to leave the area, the man begged Him to stay. For he knew the true nature of the Lord of all.

But Jesus had to refuse. He parted with these words for today—warm words of encouragement and challenge. A reminder of God's power and compassion in all our lives.

If you were to obey Jesus' word as if it had been spoken to you, what would you say? Take some time today to recount in your mind the works He has performed—or perhaps is in the midst of performing—in your life.

Why not follow in the footsteps of the demon-freed man today? Go tell your family and friends.

Who touched my clothes?

—Mark 5:30

The woman had been bleeding for twelve years. People could not touch her or be with her, or they would become ceremonially unclean as she had been all that time. She had been to many physicians seeking a cure, to no avail. The only thing her quest accomplished was to spend all her money.

Then she heard about Jesus. She told herself all she needed to do was touch Him, and if everything they said was true, she would be made whole and clean again.

In the crowd, she made her way to Him and touched His clothes. Instantly, she knew she was healed. That's when Jesus asked who touched Him.

The woman feared reprisal, but she won compassion and healing. Her faith made her well.

In the hustle and bustle of your life today, Jesus walks by. Reach for Him, and see what happens next.

Don't worry. Just have faith!

—*Mark 5:36*

Jairus was a ruler of the synagogue. Jesus had not been a very popular figure among his colleagues. And yet, when his daughter lay ill, he approached Jesus in faith.

But by the time Jesus made it to Jairus's house, his daughter had died. It was too late. Or so it seemed.

Then Jesus spoke these words. On the surface, they seem like a lightweight platitude someone might say in an effort to cheer up a downcast acquaintance. But Jesus doesn't say things like that. He means every word He speaks.

And when He tells you not to worry but to have faith, you can be sure it's a live option. And one well worth obeying.

What tough situation in your life is Jesus encouraging you to have faith in?

"Talitha, koum!" which means, "Little girl, get up!"
—Mark 5:41

The twelve-year-old girl lay still in death. But Jesus approached her in the company of His closest friends and her father and mother.

The professional mourners had laughed at Him for saying she was only sleeping. They didn't know Him or His power.

Jesus took the girl's hand and told her to get up. And she awoke from death and stood up. Healed. Whole. Alive.

The people in that room with her were overcome with amazement. Jesus asked them to keep what happened quiet and to give the girl something to eat.

Jesus accomplishes the impossible without even exerting Himself. Yet we stand overcome with amazement. How weak our faith must seem to Him. How shallow our trust.

Yet the little girl heard His voice and arose. Maybe we can, too.

If any place won't welcome you or listen to your message, leave and shake the dust from your feet as a warning to them.

—Mark 6:11

Jesus sent out a number of His followers, two by two, to share the message of the gospel in villages and towns throughout the region.

They took no food or extra clothing with them. They were dependent on people responding to them and welcoming them into their homes, which was usual behavior in that culture.

But Jesus left no doubt about how they were to treat people who didn't accept their message. Shaking the dust off one's feet was a gesture Jewish people used to express extreme contempt for or rejection of someone else.

Jesus' comments indicate the importance of hearing and heeding His Word. And the consequences for failing to do both.

Let's go to a place where we can be alone and get some rest.

—Mark 6:31

The disciples had been out in the countryside preaching. When they returned to tell their Master about what they had done and said, He spoke today's words.

No rest for the weary. No solitude for the overwhelmed, however. The people "figured out where they were going. So people from every town ran on ahead and got there first" (Mark 6:33).

Responsibilities pile up. People swarm around you, wanting more and more of your time and energy. Plans get changed, and not by you.

Still, in the midst of that seeming chaos, God is at work. And you may not be able to take Jesus' invitation literally today, but you can be alone with Him in your spirit. He will give you the heavenly rest of the soul.

How much bread do you have? Go and see!
—*Mark 6:38*

The multitude engulfed Jesus and His disciples. They were spiritually hungry, sheep without shepherd, and Jesus had great compassion upon them.

After a long day of teaching and ministering, the disciples wisely suggested that Jesus send the people away, so they could get food before they fainted from starvation.

But Jesus dumbfounded the disciples by telling them, "You give them something to eat." He forced them to look at the resources they had at hand.

Jesus took that meager amount and multiplied it to the point that basketfuls were left over.

You may be facing a task that feels overwhelming. Deep down, you know you do not have the resources required. Take stock. Count your loaves of bread. Let Jesus remove the weighty burden so you can see the situation more objectively.

DAY 265

Don't worry! I am Jesus.

—Mark 6:50

Jesus sent His disciples ahead of Him in a boat. He used the opportunity to depart to the mountain to pray.

After His refreshing time with His Father, Jesus saw the disciples in the middle of the lake. They were having trouble getting anywhere, let alone where they wanted to go, because of the brisk wind. Perhaps you know the feeling.

So He walked out to them on the water. In fact, He almost passed them by He was moving so quickly.

His figure appeared to be a ghost, and they were troubled. But Jesus identified Himself as their Friend and Master. He climbed into their boat, and the wind ceased. And they marveled.

Jesus is capable of stilling the wind that keeps you from moving forward. Listen to His greeting as if it were directed to you today. Feel the wind die down. And proceed in peace.

DAY 266

The prophet Isaiah was right when he wrote that God had said, "All of you praise me with your words, but you never really think about me. It is useless for you to worship me, when you teach rules made up by humans."

—Mark 7:6–7

Centuries ago, Isaiah the prophet brought God's message of judgment. His cold, hard words ripped through the religious facade and got to the heart of the matter. And that heart was cold and empty.

Jesus applied those words to the religious leaders of His day. Men who scrupulously followed the minutiae of religion while carefully steering clear of its meaning and purpose.

And that problem has plagued humanity ever since.

In fact, it may be a problem you're dealing with today.

Stop. Open your heart. Let it become real because it is real.

DAY 267

You disobey God's commands in order to obey what humans have taught.

—Mark 7:8

Jesus accused the men who were responsible for the spiritual lives of the nation of Israel with setting aside God's commands and replacing them with traditions established by people.

Instead of living a life of holiness, love, and grace, they had become enamored of—and encumbered by—the fine print details of ceremonial cleansings and other religious minutiae that humanity had added to the law over the years. And so they had grown distant from God and His ways. And led the people with them.

Priorities matter to God. Purposes, motives, ideals—they all spring from the heart. And if the heart is trapped by chains of nonsensical and rigid rules, it can't beat for God very long.

Free yourself to experience God, learn about Him, and express Him freely to others.

You are good at rejecting God's commands so that you can follow your own teachings!

—Mark 7:9

The last thing the religious leaders thought they were doing was rejecting God's commands, which made their situation all the more pathetic and ironic.

Elsewhere Jesus summarized the commands as loving God with the totality of your being and loving neighbors as yourself.

The heart of God's command was love. Service. Grace. Mercy. And those were the precise elements that had been squeezed out of the religion of the Pharisees by the overwhelming demands of their human tradition.

They thought they were doing right and being religious. Certainly, they must be doing God a great favor in instructing the people in their ways. But Jesus looked at the same situation from a divine perspective and saw nothing of genuine religion.

Today is a good day to look at some of your views from another perspective.

DAY 269

Didn't Moses command you to respect your father and mother? Didn't he tell you to put to death all who curse their parents?

—Mark 7:10

Jesus cites Moses' words—actually God's commands through Moses. Clear commands regarding one's duty toward parents, both positively (the fifth of the Ten Commandments) and negatively.

The law required adequate financial support and care for older parents, and it prescribed death for people who treated their parents contemptuously.

Pretty serious admonitions. And seemingly disregarded by many these days.

You know your parents were human, having had human parents themselves with all the faults and frailties that involves. And you also know that God desires not only that we honor our parents but that we forgive them. Today, honor your parents, even if that means forgiving them.

Pay attention and try to understand what I mean.
—Mark 7:14

Jesus shouts to the multitude, drawing their attention to the teaching He is about to share.

Is He shouting the same to you today?

Open your ears. And your heart. Your Lord wishes to speak to you. To teach you. To reveal His truth, His presence, His love to you.

His Word is available to all. Not just you, but everyone. No one is excluded. No one can be denied. The invitation is open to all who hear.

And He wants you to understand Him. To truly hear, from the inside out. To understand and thereby to obey.

So, what is He saying to you today? Ask Him. Hear Him. Understand Him. Obey Him.

He yearns to communicate with you.

The food that you put into your mouth does not make you unclean and unfit to worship God. The bad words that come out of your mouth are what make you unclean.

—Mark 7:15–16

Jesus pointed out rather forcefully that—at least morally speaking—a person is defiled not by anything from the outside but by things from the inside. From the core of the person. From the soul.

The source of true defilement is found within, not without. And all the business about washing hands that preoccupied the religious leaders only camouflaged the true issues. The religious leaders got stuck with the hands and let the heart go uncleansed.

It's easy to wash the soil off the hands. It's much harder to deal with the soiled soul—the pain and sin that keep us from living as we really want to.

Are you getting sidetracked by petty issues and ignoring the serious matters of your life? What steps could you take to deal with them?

DAY 272

Out of your heart come evil thoughts, vulgar deeds, stealing, murder, unfaithfulness in marriage, greed, meanness, deceit, indecency, envy, insults, pride, and foolishness.

—Mark 7:21–22

To the religious leaders, Jesus recounts the kinds of evil that seem to pour out of the human heart.

To read this morning's newspaper is to witness stark evidence that very little has changed since Jesus' day.

We would much prefer to think that our interiors are clean and pure and innocent and free. But Jesus reminds us that the human heart is the source of all kinds of sinful, hurtful, destructive behavior.

Deep down, we know that's true. And we must accept it in order to deal with it.

Take an honest look at yourself. Perhaps there are some items in this list you'd call your own. Confront them head-on. Jesus understands. And He still loves you.

The children must first be fed! It isn't right to take away their food and feed it to dogs.

—Mark 7:27

A Greek woman from Syro-Phoenicia approached Jesus, asking Him to heal her demon-possessed daughter. His answer surprises many with its forthrightness.

But Jesus was explaining as directly as He could that His primary priority while on earth was to work with and teach His disciples, Jews. The woman was a Gentile.

Even so, the woman's faith caused her to persist in her request. She said that even the dogs get to eat the crumbs the children drop under the table.

Thanks to the woman's persistence, her daughter was healed by Jesus' power.

Jesus knew His purpose. And yet He was also willing to be open to opportunities to serve— even if they fell outside that purpose.

That's a good model to follow today.

"Effatha!" which means "Open up!"
—*Mark 7:34*

Jesus went to the Sea of Galilee to minister. People brought a man to Him who was deaf and could barely speak.

Jesus took the man aside by himself. Through putting His fingers in the man's ear, touching his tongue, and looking toward heaven, Jesus communicated what He was about to do for the man.

Jesus sighed deeply, perhaps out of compassion or weariness. And He said to the man an Aramaic word that means "be completely opened." And he was.

Let the language of heaven speak to you. Then utter it to others.

Today, you may be feeling closed down, unable to sense much of anything. From yourself, from others, from God.

Let Jesus remove the things that hinder you from hearing Him speak to you. Let Him remove the impediment to your free speech on His behalf.

Why are you always looking for a sign? I can promise you that you will not be given one!

—Mark 8:12

Mark tells us that Jesus sighed deeply in His spirit just before He said these words. He was deeply distressed at the stubborn unbelief of the people of Israel, the so-called children of God, and especially of their religious leaders.

Why must they have a sign? Why couldn't they just accept Jesus for who He was in childlike faith?

With a touch of anger, Jesus made clear His intentions: There would be no sign for that people.

There's nothing wrong with asking for supernatural validation as long as it arises out of the faith of the one asking for it. But when the request comes out of unbelief, it's not worthy of consideration. Are you asking Jesus for some kind of sign? Consider where that request is coming from.

DAY 276

Are your eyes blind and your ears deaf? Don't you remember?

—Mark 8:18

Blindness. Deafness. And very poor memories. The disciples of Jesus seemed plagued by such problems—at least spiritually.

They were living with Jesus in their very midst, witnessing His daily miracles, hearing Him preach before small groups in homes and multitudes on the hillside. Laughing with Him, crying with Him, walking and teasing and fishing. And still they had trouble understanding what was happening right under their noses.

Frankly, their lack of understanding is a bit consoling. We can feel better about our lack of comprehension of spiritual truths.

Obviously, Jesus demands a lot of His followers. He expects us to grow and mature and learn and develop. And He may even get a bit impatient with our progress. But it reveals His deep, intense love for His own. It proves He wants only the very best for us.

OCTOBER 2

Don't you know what I am talking about by now?
—Mark 8:21

Jesus recalled for the disciples two miraculous meals—feeding the five thousand and the four thousand from just a few loaves of bread and some fish.

Their failure to understand *what* happened seemed to show they really didn't understand *why* it happened, either. And by not understanding the *why*, they really didn't understand *who* Jesus was and what He was about.

That grieved the Lord. He deeply wanted His closest followers to understand.

Sometimes we get things rather quickly. Sometimes it takes a time or two or ten for God to click some truth into the consciousness. And too many times it takes a lifetime to understand.

We need to be alert, prepared, open, ready. And when we are, understanding will come in its own good time.

What could you give to get back your soul?
—*Mark 8:37*

It all comes down to this: Nothing, absolutely nothing, is worth losing your soul over.

Possessions. Pleasures. Passions. Power. Nothing is more important than cultivating the spiritual life.

We can look at the work we produce with our hands, and we can rely on success to give us happiness. We can enjoy the things we buy that give us pleasure and comfort and escape, and they can seem important to our well-being. We can even be with our families and friends, and we can realize that life is good with good relationships. And sometimes that can seem to be enough.

But the spiritual life, taking care of the soul, is much more elusive to understand and appreciate. It can't be seen. Yet it is the ultimate reality.

Don't be ashamed of me and my message among these unfaithful and sinful people! If you are, the Son of Man will be ashamed of you when he comes in the glory of his Father with the holy angels.

—*Mark 8:38*

Look at what Jesus is saying today. It's an if-then situation: If you're ashamed of Jesus and His words, then He will be ashamed of you.

If you love and serve Him and walk with Him in faith and trust, open to His message and desiring to follow it, then there is no shame.

So which path are you on? If you have shame about the fact that you are a Christian, then how could Jesus not feel the same?

But that's not where you are today. Your heart is right. It is open. It is obedient. There is no shame in loving Jesus. He has no shame with you.

That thought can certainly encourage you until the day He comes again.

I promise you that some of the people standing here will not die before they see God's kingdom come with power.

—Mark 9:1

Jesus was speaking of Peter, James, and John, who journeyed with Him six days later up a mountainside. There they caught a fantastic glimpse of the kingdom of God in all its power, seeing Jesus in all His glory along with Elijah and Moses.

The kingdom of God had ripped through the fabric of time and space and was present on that mountaintop. It was quite an experience for those disciples.

Mountaintop experiences can give us energy, peace, and a sense of excitement and purpose. But we, like the disciples, must come back to earth.

When you do, take a little of the kingdom's glory with you. Look back on those times of wonderful joy and freedom, and gain encouragement during your times in the valley.

That's why Jesus shared that glimpse of the kingdom with His closest followers. And why He can do the same for you today.

Anything is possible for someone who has faith!
—Mark 9:23

A man spoke up out of the multitude to Jesus. His son was possessed of a spirit that caused him to convulse. The boy was brought to the Lord, and he immediately fell to the ground, shaking violently.

Jesus asked the man how long his son had suffered so. "From childhood," the man answered. "Please have pity and help us if you can!" (Mark 9:22).

A note of doubt. After all, the boy had suffered for years. How could anything change now?

But Jesus responded with today's words. You see, it's not Jesus' power that should be questioned but the man's faith.

The man cried out, "I do have faith! Please help me to have even more."

Maybe that should be your prayer today.

I order you to come out of the boy! Don't ever bother him again.

—*Mark 9:25*

The boy who had been inhabited by an evil spirit lay before Jesus, convulsing, thrashing, out of control.

Jesus spoke directly and forcefully to the spirit, commanding him to come out and never enter again.

The departure was violent. It seemed the boy was left for dead. But Jesus took his weak hand and pulled him up. He was freed from the bondage of the evil spirit forever.

The word of Jesus Christ is irresistible, irrevocable. It changes things. Forever.

The spirit world acknowledges that. Evil spirits have no choice but to obey Him.

Yet you have been given a will. You seem to have a choice. What command of the King of the universe are you wrestling with today?

DAY 283

Only prayer can force out that kind of demon.
—Mark 9:29

The disciples were embarrassed. Frustrated. A father had come to them with his demon-possessed son and asked them to free him from the evil spirit or else he could be physically destroyed. They failed. The evil spirit ignored their demands.

But the evil spirit immediately obeyed Jesus' command.

What was the difference? The disciples came to Jesus privately and asked Him why they couldn't cast the demon out.

Jesus answered with today's reading. Some demons are more powerful than others. And to deal with them, we must be prepared by prayer.

You may not be asked to cast out a demon today. But you will certainly be faced with any number of challenges, problems, heartaches, and confusing options in life. You can be prepared to face them in faith.

OCTOBER 9

[Jesus] was teaching the disciples that the Son of Man would be handed over to people who would kill him. But three days later he would rise to life.

—*Mark 9:31*

It was the second time Jesus foretold His death to His disciples. And He injected an ominous note: betrayal.

That betrayal was happening as He spoke. He knew what plans were being plotted in Judas's heart. And still He pressed on.

The news would ultimately be good. He would be killed, yes. But He would rise again.

Perhaps you've been betrayed. You may want to look at how Jesus handled His betrayal by Judas. He accepted it. As painful as it was. And as serious as it would become.

Maybe that's the step you need to take today. To accept it, and move forward. He will help you.

When you welcome even a child because of me, you welcome me. And when you welcome me, you welcome the one who sent me.

—*Mark 9:37*

In Jesus' day, a child was insignificant. Unimportant. Easily ignored. A child's views weren't taken seriously. The feelings were mere trifles that should be shaken off.

To be sure, despite advances in understanding children and their needs and behavior, not much has changed. The same is true whether you consider actual children, yours or others', or the child within. The hurting child, the playful child, the needy child, within you or within others.

Jesus says, welcome a little child, and you welcome Jesus.

Welcome Jesus, and you welcome the Father.

Look for the children today. Welcome each one you meet with love and joy. And revel in your reward.

Don't stop him! No one who works miracles in my name will soon turn and say something bad about me.

—Mark 9:39

Some of the disciples encountered a man who was casting out demons in the name of Jesus. Yet, he wasn't one of them, one of the Twelve. He wasn't even a regular follower of Jesus.

Proudly, the disciple John and the others forbade the man to use Jesus' name. Perhaps John expected commendation for his action. That certainly wasn't what he got.

The truth was, the man must have been a true follower of Jesus if he was performing miracles in His name.

All believers are to be tolerant of other believers, no matter what their traditions or styles of worship. If it's done in the name of Jesus, according to the will of God, that is enough. The way is open for people to follow Jesus and to serve Him as they are called and empowered and directed. That's God's way. It's the way of love and grace. Let it be your way today, too.

Anyone who is not against us is for us.

—*Mark 9:40*

Jesus opens wide the door of fellowship.

After John complained of a man who was not one of them, yet who cast out demons in Jesus' name, the Lord made it clear that His way is inclusive, not exclusive.

Our attitude is usually that people have to be strongly *for* us, or we don't include them. But Jesus gives people the benefit of the doubt. He says those who are *not against* us are for us.

You probably know several people who are strong in their faith, actively seeking and serving God. You also no doubt know a few who may be hostile to Christianity and have made it clear they're not interested. But do you know people who don't seem opposed to the idea but never really considered it?

Jesus says they can be part of "us." Take an opportunity today to reach out to someone you know like that. It may make all the difference in the world to that person.

Anyone who gives you a cup of water in my name, just because you belong to me, will surely be rewarded.

—Mark 9:41

Serving is one thing. We know we need to do it. We want to do it. We are fulfilled by doing it. And we know we will be rewarded for it.

But being served by others makes some of us a bit uncomfortable.

Sometimes we think we're helping the people who offer us a gift of service by turning them down, making it easier for them. Sometimes we think we don't deserve to receive a loving act of service from someone else. Sometimes we think it's really not important. We don't realize the sacrifice someone may be making to serve us.

These attitudes may look good on the surface. But Jesus says these attitudes rob the other person of the reward. Anyone who serves you in Jesus' name, because you are one of His, will be rewarded.

And that can be a wonderful thing to be part of.

Everyone must be salted with fire.
—Mark 9:49

Fire purifies, cleanses, cures.

Salt seasons, preserves, flavors.

To be a disciple of Jesus, a genuine follower of the Lord, one must endure the fire of pain and suffering to become the salt of the earth.

To have a preserving, seasoning, thirst-creating impact in the world, one must have been taken through the cleansing fire that purifies. That doesn't sound easy. Or desirable.

Thank God, it isn't, or it wouldn't be worth doing.

Thank God, too, that He is with you every step of the way.

And thank God, yet again, that the end result is eternal fulfillment.

It is far better to experience and grow through the painful fire that can come as a result of being a faithful follower of Christ than to face the fiery torment of eternal life without Him.

Salt is good. But if it no longer tastes like salt, how can it be made salty again? Have salt among you and live at peace with each other.

—Mark 9:50

Salt is good, Jesus says. But unsalty salt is worthless. You can't make it salty again. It's mere bland crystals.

Jesus desires that His followers be salty. The salt of the earth.

But the term *salty* has gained, ironically, a rather unsavory reputation as a character trait these days. It can mean coarse, rough around the edges, profane.

That's not likely what Jesus has in mind. He's thinking of salt's preserving qualities. It keeps things from rotting.

He's thinking of its thirst-causing function. It makes people want the Water of Life.

He's thinking of its seasoning and flavoring. It adds depth and meaning to life.

And when you're salty in these ways, you're naturally at peace with each other.

But in the beginning God made a man and a
woman.

—Mark 10:6

What is a man? How should a woman live?
These have been troubling questions since the
beginning of time. Yet the answers seem less clear
than ever.

Jesus says, from the beginning, that God created two distinct genders. He made a man and a
woman. Both are human. Both have essential
similarities. But the differences can be vast.

Yes, men can learn from women, and vice
versa. But it seems our society is bent on homog-
enizing the genders into one. It just won't work.
Our brains are different; our desires are different;
our manner of living is different.

We can celebrate and enjoy the differences.
But we can recognize them and refuse to force
them into something they can't be.

What issues are you dealing with in this arena
today? Pray about them. Accept God's truth.
And thank Him for the differences.

You know the commandments. "Do not murder. Be faithful in marriage. Do not steal. Do not tell lies about others. Do not cheat. Respect your father and mother."

—Mark 10:19

As Jesus walked down the road, a man ran toward Him, knelt before Him, and asked, "Good teacher, what can I do to have eternal life?" (Mark 10:17).

Jesus gave the obvious answer, for good Jews knew the commandments and followed them. He offered a quick overview of the Ten Commandments. And the man answered, "Teacher, I have obeyed . . . since I was a young man" (Mark 10:20).

Jesus knew from looking at him that he was wealthy. He saw deep within the man's soul.

The man seemed to be sincere in his desire to have eternal life. But his outward obedience to the law hadn't really reached his heart.

Is there something blocking your way to an open, honest, eternal relationship with God?

There's one thing you still need to do. Go sell everything you own. Give the money to the poor, and you will have riches in heaven. Then come with me.

—*Mark 10:21*

Jesus looked at the rich young man lovingly and said he needed to do one more thing. His obedience had been complete but perhaps not heartfelt. If it had been, it would have influenced his life totally. He needed to sell what he had and give the money to the poor. Then he would have "riches in heaven."

The man was crestfallen. He went away sad, for he had great possessions. If he intended to do what Jesus had said, he wouldn't have been so sorrowful. It was a major blockage to the eternal life he sought.

Each of us must face the same kind of decision the rich young man faced. What would happen if you had to decide today?

It's hard for rich people to get into God's kingdom!
—Mark 10:23

The rich young man had just walked away from Jesus and His followers, crushed in spirit because of his allegiance to his possessions. And Jesus used the opportunity to teach His disciples.

To the Jews, wealth was a sign that God had blessed them. Therefore, it was difficult to understand the concept that riches could hinder one's entrance into the kingdom of God. That's why the disciples were astonished at Jesus' words.

Too many rich people trust in their riches. There's not much trust left for God.

It's easy to fall into the trap of trusting money and possessions to gain satisfaction and comfort and security. Where's your trust today? What's keeping you from placing your trust where you want it? How can you overcome that?

[They] will make fun of him and spit on him. They will beat him and kill him. But three days later he will rise to life.

—*Mark 10:34*

For the third time in Mark's gospel, Jesus announces His death and resurrection. But this time He adds further details about how it will happen.

He and His disciples were traveling to Jerusalem. There He would be mocked and belittled. He, the King of the universe! The Son of God who is worthy of all praise and honor! Reduced to being made fun of by pitiful humans.

He would be spat upon. The ultimate indignity. The deepest humiliation.

He would be beaten. A painfully abusive torture involving whips and sharp rocks, ripping the skin off His very human back.

And He would be killed.

Even so, He traveled to Jerusalem. Because He knew it was His destiny.

What He asks of you pales in comparison. Don't sidestep. Whatever He tells you to do, do it.

Jesus asked them what they wanted.
—Mark 10:36

James and John made a rather bold request of Jesus: "Teacher, will you do us a favor?" (Mark 10:35). So He asked them what they wanted Him to do.

They wanted to sit by Him in the two highest seats of honor in heaven. He turned them down because it wasn't His decision but the Father's.

Jesus' communication style can teach us how to relate to others who request time or attention.

First, get clear about the request. Next, carefully evaluate the request. Is it in your power to grant? Is it something you can give freely? Then, explain your answer directly. And as fully as you can.

Be honest, clear, direct, yet loving.

My house should be called a place of worship for all nations.

—Mark 11:17

In His anger with the religious leaders, who had turned the temple of God into an unsavory five-and-dime, Jesus quoted a verse from the prophet Isaiah. It's from a section wherein God speaks of the day when His salvation is extended to all people, no matter what nation they represent. Not just the Jews.

Everyone will be welcome. All can enjoy the benefits of grace and mercy. All can proclaim the praises of God together, side by side.

What Jesus found in the capital was far from this picture. Not only were the Jews totally exclusive, but the place of worship had become the haunt of fast-buck artists, scam masters, and cheats. And the religious leaders were profiting from it all. The people profited not a bit. The situation angered Jesus.

If we see situations like the one Jesus faced, we should be angered, too.

Have faith in God!
—Mark 11:22

The disciples had witnessed an astonishing display of Christ's power: Days earlier, He had cursed a fig tree. Today, it was barren and withered.

Peter pointed out the tree's condition, and Jesus responded with these words: "Have faith in God! If you have faith in God and don't doubt, you can tell this mountain to get up and jump into the sea, and it will. Everything you ask for in prayer will be yours, if you only have faith" (Mark 11:22–24).

Even if it's a withered fig tree.

It's a strange lesson. It seems Jesus had a fit of temper, He cursed the tree, and it died. But Jesus used it to show the power of faith.

It's faith in God. So the act performed in faith must fall within the realm of God's will.

What would you do with that kind of faith?

Everything you ask for in prayer will be yours, if you only have faith.

—Mark 11:24

Faith isn't something we think. Faith isn't the words we say. Faith isn't something that comes automatically. Rather, faith comes from deeply rooted convictions of the heart.

Jesus says to ask for things when you pray. It's an invitation. When you ask, He says it will be yours if you have faith.

Sounds simple enough. But how often do you experience it happening this way?

That's where faith comes in. It's the utter, abandoned trust in God that empowers us. It's an absolute confidence in what we say and ask for because we know the will of God. And we know the will of God because we are so close to Him.

That's where faith starts. Close to God. Soaking in His glory.

DAY 300

Whenever you stand up to pray, you must forgive what others have done to you. Then your Father in heaven will forgive your sins.

—Mark 11:25

Effective prayer requires an open line of communication. A line unhindered by jealousies, hurts, grievances, and any other wrong inflicted on you by any other person.

Unless you clear up that line, your prayer has a difficult time getting through because your heart's not in it. It can't be. It's too busy eating itself up with painful hurts.

If you have anything against anyone—and Jesus leaves no room there to wiggle out of it—forgive. Drop your clenched fists. Open your hands to the Lord.

Only then can He really hear you. Only then can you honestly share your prayers with your Lord. And only then can He in turn forgive you for your sins.

Do whatever you must do today to start the process of forgiveness in your life.

But if you do not forgive, neither will your Father in heaven forgive your trespasses.

—Mark 11:26 NKJV

You have every right to be upset with that person. You were mistreated. Harmed. Deeply hurt. You did nothing to deserve the treatment you received. You would be within your rights to try to get back at that person.

Anyone in your situation would feel the same way. It's only human. Even if it happened long ago, it's still a grievous wrong against you. If only God would do something to that person.

All these statements may be true. But listen to what Jesus says today.

Forgiveness is not an option to the one who desires an intimate, open relationship with God. God has forgiven you. And you didn't deserve it. You can forgive others, even those who don't deserve it, because you deserve a clean slate.

You are completely wrong! You don't know what the Scriptures teach. And you don't know anything about the power of God.

—Mark 12:24

The Sadducees asked Jesus a question to test Him. But He saw right through them, for they asked a question about the resurrection, which they didn't even believe in.

Jesus called them on it. He said, in effect, "You don't know what you're talking about because you know neither the Scriptures nor the power of God. If you did, you wouldn't believe as you do."

Jesus went on to explain His answer to their question, but He certainly wasn't intimidated. He was confident in the truth. It is, after all, truth that creates confidence. God's truth. The kind of truth you could stake your life on, which is precisely what Jesus would ultimately do.

When you are confident in the truth, you can stand in strength against any challenge.

You are not far from God's kingdom.
—Mark 12:34

A religious leader questioned Jesus concerning the greatest commandment. Jesus answered that the first was to love God with heart, soul, mind, and strength, and the second was to love your neighbor as yourself.

The scribe responded that loving God and others as you love yourself is more than all the rigid structure of rules that the leaders had constructed around the basic law of God. He had a way to go, but he was on the right track.

It was a wise answer, and Jesus knew it. So He made today's statement. Certainly, the man wasn't far from the kingdom; he was in the presence of Jesus Himself, who brought the kingdom to humanity.

Today, you're not far from the kingdom, either. You're well on your way. You're in the presence of the King.

You may have a way to go, but the King is walking with you. Take comfort in that.

I tell you that this poor widow has put in more than all the others. Everyone else gave what they didn't need. But she is very poor and gave everything she had. Now she doesn't have a cent to live on.

—Mark 12:43–44

Jesus sat in the temple, people-watching. He sat across from the treasury, where people put their offerings into large trumpet-shaped receptacles.

There were all kinds of people. Rich who gave much. Rich who gave little. Poor who gave nothing. And one poor widow who offered two mites—a fraction of a penny. Hardly worth worrying about.

Yet Jesus noted that she had given more than any because she gave all she had.

Giving is a personal matter between you and God. But the status of your giving should tell you how well your relationship with Him is going. Giving flows out of a thankful heart. An obedient heart. A heart that overflows with love.

Nations and kingdoms will go to war against each other. There will be earthquakes in many places, and people will starve to death. But this is just the beginning of troubles.

—*Mark 13:8*

The beginning of troubles. Birth pains for the end of time.

Jesus offers clues to when that time will be. Nations and kingdoms battling. Earthquakes and famines growing in intensity and frequency.

It's not a comforting picture unless you realize that it means God's perfect plan is being realized. And as a child of God, you will be spared His wrath toward sin.

Some people say this description sounds like today. Perhaps we are entering the end times. If so, we need to prepare ourselves—and our loved ones—for that time. But if not, we need to continue doing what we're doing. Growing. Struggling. Reaching out. Praying. Working. One day at a time.

The good news must be preached to all nations.
—*Mark 13:10*

Jesus revealed some fascinating insights to His disciples about the end times, the final days before the culmination of history. But first, He noted, the good news must be preached to all nations.

That information must have been a bit of a shock to His Jewish disciples. They were used to having a religion that was exclusive. A religion that even looked down on the "pagan" peoples around them. The Messiah was coming as *their* Savior. Or so they thought.

Jesus had to expand their vision because He had come for the whole world. And that message had to be shared with the whole world.

That's why we have missionaries, who sacrifice and struggle to share the love of God with anyone. You may not be a missionary, but you can be part of the process just by letting God's love shine through you to others. Whoever they may be.

When you are arrested, don't worry about what you will say. You will be given the right words when the time comes. But you will not really be the ones speaking. Your words will come from the Holy Spirit.

—Mark 13:11

Polish your image. Be prepared. You'd better look good. You'd better look like you know what you're talking about, even if you don't. Bluff your way to success.

That's the way of the world. Businesses are made or broken on presentation skills.

Jesus says, throw all that out. When you're up against the wall for His sake, because of your faith, don't worry. Don't think out what you're going to say.

Just trust Him, and speak because the Holy Spirit, not you, will be speaking.

Jesus is ready to speak and act through you, no matter what situation you find yourself in.

But be on your guard! That's why I am telling you these things now.

—Mark 13:23

Having the curtain pulled back on the future and seeing it all at once in its terrifying glory can be a bit overwhelming.

That's what Jesus did with His disciples. He revealed the struggles and the pains humankind must face in those final days.

But He did so for a reason: to urge His followers to be on their guard. To take heed. To know what to expect. And to live in light of it.

This way, there are really no surprises, at least as long as we listen to what Jesus has said. He has told us everything we need to know well ahead of time.

How are you responding to it? Is it helping to energize your walk with Him, keep your priorities straight, and maintain your focus on what He's called you to do?

He will send his angels to gather his chosen ones from all over the earth.

—Mark 13:27

Fantastic. Unbelievable. Astonishing. But they're Jesus' words.

In the final day, the Father will send forth His angels to travel to every area of the world to gather His children and bring them to Himself.

That's the desire of the Father, to have us all in His presence to delight in forever. And that's precisely what will happen someday.

We don't know exactly how it will happen. And we certainly don't know when.

But don't get bogged down in details. Meditate on the main point: God will bring you home, into His presence, no matter where you are. Because He wants you. Because He loves you.

And that is what all of history is heading toward. Think about that.

DAY 310

So when you see all these things happening, you will know that the time has almost come.

—Mark 13:29

Time and again, Jesus revealed truths about the day He would return in glory. And the lesson, time and again, was to be ready.

What does that mean? Does it mean living a perfect life? Certainly not. Jesus understands our humanity.

Does it mean keeping ourselves free from the world, staying safe at home, waiting? Not at all. Jesus wants us to be out in the world, living and loving as He would, and thereby drawing others into the kingdom with us.

Being ready means staying on the path of healthy growth—spiritually and emotionally. Taking each day as a gift, one at a time, and being open to His will. Living as fully and richly as you can as His child. Follow that plan, and you'll be ready.

I tell everyone just what I have told you. Be on your guard!

—Mark 13:37

Be on your guard!"

That doesn't mean be paranoid. That doesn't mean fear the future or the present. That doesn't mean spend your time squinting into the future, trying to forecast it or figure it out.

That means be aware of what's happening around you. Not only personally, but in your family, your friends, your fellowship, your community, your nation, your world.

Keep up to date. Be informed. Be knowledgeable of the needs and trends of life around you because it's all pointing in one direction: the future.

We know what the future holds. And who holds it.

As you watch and stay on your guard, you can take comfort that God is working out His purposes. Don't fear. Trust God.

She has done all she could by pouring perfume on my body to prepare it for burial.

—Mark 14:8

The woman who anointed Jesus with oil expressed deep devotion to her Lord. It was a simple act, yet costly: The ointment stirred a debate among the disciples about whether the money for it had been wasted by the act. It was also bold and daring. The woman was even rebuked harshly for what she did.

But Jesus set them straight. He received the act as a token of love and adoration. A foretaste of His anointing in death for burial. An anointing that would never, as it turns out, be necessary.

The only anointing He would receive pointed to His death, and in its glorious worship, it hinted at His resurrection.

The woman did a simple act of obedient service. Willingly, whatever the cost. And she remains an example for us today.

The one who will betray me is now eating with me.
—*Mark 14:18*

Imagine spending three years of your life with a Man whose vision and love captured you. Times of excitement and exhaustion, of travel and travail.

Imagine being a witness to miracles we tend to take for granted today.

Imagine developing bonds of friendship and brotherhood with eleven others. Laughing, bickering, working together, praying, learning, fearing, risking.

And now imagine your Leader revealing that one among you would betray Him.

How could it be? Who would do such a thing? And why?

Unfortunately, every one of us will betray our Lord at one time or another. Certainly not on the scale that Judas did. But by living in a way that denies His power or His presence in our lives, we're denying Him.

Thank God, Jesus understands. And forgives. And accepts. And heals.

All of you will reject me, as the Scriptures say, "I will strike down the shepherd, and the sheep will be scattered."

—*Mark 14:27*

The Shepherd will be slaughtered; the sheep will be scattered. And as a result, they will stumble and fall because of their relationship with Him.

The disciples would face a severe loss, and it would affect them greatly. Perhaps they were glad at least to know it was coming, so they could prepare for it as best they could.

Even so, it's a lesson for us: From time to time, life will throw us some wicked punches. The impact may be shattering to our emotions. So we must be prepared spiritually and emotionally to confront whatever comes our way.

The good news is, it's all part of God's plan for us. It will be resolved. And ultimately, it will be good. These thoughts can bring some measure of comfort in the process. You have Someone to turn to who is waiting to give you support.

But after I am raised to life, I will go ahead of you to Galilee.

—Mark 14:28

Did the fact that Jesus would be raised from the dead really sink in to the disciples' minds? Judging by their surprise on the Resurrection morning, it doesn't seem to have. Yet Jesus talks of it matter-of-factly.

Yes, He faces death. But He will be raised to life. And He will go ahead of them to Galilee.

Today, Jesus still goes before us. He sets out on the path and prepares the way.

So to follow in the direction we feel led to take personally is to follow in His footsteps. And we can trust that whatever happens is His will when we obey Him, for He has gone before us. And He has done so in His resurrected power and authority.

As you face today, what have you to fear? Why do you worry about the direction you're taking? Take it a step at a time. Because they're His steps, too.

This very night before a rooster crows twice, you
will say three times that you don't know me.

—Mark 14:30

Hory can that be? Everyone else may fall away,
but not me, Peter defiantly tells his Lord.

But Jesus sets His friend straight. Oh, you'll
fall away all right. In fact, this very night you'll
deny Me not once but three times.

There's no trace of shame and hurt; Jesus simply points out a fact to Peter. It's part of the
process, part of the plan. For Peter, it had to have
been an incredibly painful part.

Jesus knows what you're thinking. He knows
your true priorities. He knows what will happen
with you when push comes to shove. And He
knows that He may be the One you deny in
times of stress or trouble or doubt or fear. But He
still loved Peter. And He still loves you.

DAY 317

Father, you can do anything. Don't make me suffer by having me drink from this cup. But do what you want, and not what I want.

—Mark 14:36

Mark's account tells us that Jesus was full of fear because of what He faced: Mockery. Abuse. Death. And absolute separation from His Father.

But His prayer offers us some guidance when we find ourselves afraid and alone.

He recognized God's power. Whatever happens, happens because God has ordained it and carried it out. His prayer was directed toward the Father purposefully and confidently.

He made a direct request: "Get Me out of this situation." Jesus was honest about how He felt.

He ultimately yielded to the Father's will. And He left the results to God.

DAY 318

I am! . . . Soon you will see the Son of Man sitting at the right side of God All-Powerful, and coming with the clouds of heaven.

—Mark 14:62

The high priest put it right to Jesus: "Are you the Messiah, the Son of the glorious God?" (Mark 14:61). And after first ignoring the question, Jesus answered directly, "I am!"

Of course, His answer was blasphemous to the religious leaders. How could He claim to be the Son of God? Unless, of course, He was.

But that option never occurred to the leaders because it threatened their position. And yet, what position could stand in the face of the Son of God?

Jesus also described how He will be seen in the future. But it made no difference to the high priest. His mind was slammed shut to the truth.

Close-mindedness can kill the spirit.

At Jesus' invitation, open your mind, your heart, and your soul to Him today.

Go and preach the good news to everyone in the world. Anyone who believes me and is baptized will be saved. But anyone who refuses to believe me will be condemned.

—Mark 16:15–16

The resurrected Christ has His eyes set on the world. And there He encourages His disciples to go.

There are no limits to the good news. The gospel is for everyone. It's easy, however, to get boxed up into our own culture, our own ethnic group, our own set ways, our own pet beliefs. And as we do, the "world" gets smaller and smaller. Our eyes become more and more near-sighted.

That's not Jesus' way. His eyes scan the far horizons, seeking those who need to hear.

We can go. We can send others through financial gifts. We can pray. But we shouldn't keep our focus too tight.

The whole world. Every creature. God's heart is that big. Yours can be, too.

John baptized with water, but in a few days you will be baptized with the Holy Spirit.

—Acts 1:5

The risen Lord met with His gathered disciples one last time. He told them to wait for the promise of the Father. The promise of a life of power and purpose, a life in the Spirit. And He distinguished the baptism of water, such as John performed, and the baptism of the Spirit, which awaited them not many days away.

It was a new day. A new kind of relationship with God awaited them—something no other believer had ever experienced before. God would be present within them.

The same Spirit moves today across the turbulent waters of your life. He dwells within, awaiting release to offer power, peace, and purpose. Moment by moment.

As a child of God, you can experience the presence of the Holy Spirit. It's yours for the asking today.

DAY 321

You don't need to know the time of those events that only the Father controls.

—Acts 1:7

Their Lord and Savior had faced death and conquered it. In His resurrection body, He stood before them, telling them of the coming of the Spirit.

Imagine the awe, the fear, the excitement, and the sadness they must have been feeling. Surely their hearts overflowed. It seemed the perfect time for the Messiah to inaugurate His kingdom on earth. After all, He stood before them, risen from the dead!

Was it indeed the time? Would He establish His kingdom?

No. Not yet. That's up to God. And His timing is perfect.

The waiting creates a tension that gives energy and keeps us reaching for more, for better, along the way. It's a life-giving tension. And it leads to a deeper life.

NOVEMBER 16

But the Holy Spirit will come upon you and give you power. Then you will tell everyone about me in Jerusalem, in all Judea, in Samaria, and everywhere in the world.

—Acts 1:8

Power. What would you do if you had all you needed? What would life be like?

Many people lust after personal power to the point that it consumes them. You see it in business. In relationships. In churches. But that's not the kind of power Jesus is talking about.

He's talking about genuine, godly power that comes to us through the Holy Spirit in our lives. An energizing, releasing, cleansing power that enables us to live more fully and love more liberally God's way.

This power has a purpose: to enable us to be His witnesses.

How powerful are you today? How far have you gone as His witness?

Saul! Saul! Why are you so cruel to me?
—*Acts 9:4*

Saul—a leading Jew—had been appalled by the radical followers of the man Jesus. He followed the Christians to their meetings, threatening to kill them.

Saul decided to go to Damascus to see if any rebels were there, determined to bring them back as prisoners to Jerusalem. Only he experienced something of a detour on the way.

Near Damascus, a light shone on him from heaven. He fell to the ground and heard a voice. Saul, in terror, asked, "Who are you?" The answer came, "I am Jesus . . . the one you are so cruel to" (Acts 9:5).

But Jesus had died, arisen, and been taken to heaven. What had Saul done to Him? As Saul had persecuted the church, he had persecuted her Lord.

Jesus identified Himself so much with His body of followers that He hurt. That's how much He identifies with you, too.

I will show him how much he must suffer for worshiping in my name.

—Acts 9:16

A Damascan disciple named Ananias was tapped by Jesus to find Saul, pray for him, lay hands on him, and heal him of his temporary blindness.

Ananias had some doubts. Imagine the fear he must have felt. Jesus wanted him to visit the man who had been harming Christians?

But the Lord assured him and added today's words.

Saul, as Paul the apostle, would indeed face torture, shipwreck, imprisonment, and much more in his quest for the gospel. It came with the territory.

You may not hear Jesus' voice audibly as Ananias did. But you may get a sense of leading from the Spirit within. Don't feel bad if your initial response is to question Him about it. He'll let you know His will. Like Ananias, obey what you know He is asking you.

Peter, get up! Kill these and eat them.
—*Acts 10:13*

Peter the apostle had gone to the roof to pray. And he fell asleep and saw a vision of heaven opening, a sheet bound at the four corners descending to him, let down to the earth: "In it were all kinds of animals, snakes, and birds" (Acts 10:12). All of them were forbidden by strict Jewish dietary law.

Then the voice of Jesus broke in to Peter's reverie. Did Peter obey? Not at all. He was still Peter: "Lord, I can't do that!" He was still obedient to the rigid rules of his former faith.

But Jesus was bringing a new way of freedom in the Spirit, of obedience to Him, not to a lot of proscribed, human-devised regulations.

What has you distracted and tied up? What do you think Jesus would say about that to you today? Ask Him.

When God says that something can be used for food, don't say it isn't fit to eat.

—Acts 10:15

The risen Jesus spoke directly to Peter in prayer, revealing three times that what Peter formerly considered out of bounds was no longer considered out of bounds by God.

The vision focused on what one could and couldn't eat according to Jewish law. But Peter learned that God had a different point of view. An open one.

But get beyond the issue of food. It's a metaphor for something else much more dramatic: people.

God opened up the world to Peter, and to all the followers of Christ. Jesus came as the Savior of the whole world.

It was a timely lesson, for a man who was not a Jew sought Peter's aid. Peter was summoned to the home of a Roman, and he went.

We can learn from Peter's willingness to minister to the Roman.

Don't be afraid to keep on preaching. Don't stop! I am with you, and you won't be harmed. Many people in this city belong to me.

—Acts 18:9–10

Paul the transformed, the Apostle of Christ, had settled into Corinth, laboring as a tentmaker, teaching and reasoning at the synagogue, persuading both Jews and Gentiles of the work of Christ.

Opposition arose, threats were made, yet he stood strong.

Still, Jesus spoke to Paul in a vision to comfort and encourage him. And these words can comfort you today.

Reread each phrase slowly. Hear it. Savor it. Accept it. Soak in it. Draw strength from the realization that you are not alone. You are part of the body of Christ. There is a vast, unbreakable network of believers around you, serving in a sense as a spiritual net to catch you if you fall.

Do you need to reach out to that body and ask for encouragement and support?

More blessings come from giving than from receiving.

—Acts 20:35

Paul quoted these words as he preached to the Ephesians about money and giving.

But they're true about more than money. They're true about your time and your energy and your effort. It's the way of the Lord. To receive spiritual strength and substance, and to turn around and give them away.

These are times you will be on the receiving end of someone's generosity. And you know what a blessing that can be.

But Jesus says to be on the giving end is even more blessed because it's following in the example of the Lord Himself, who gave all He had totally, freely, utterly. Just for us.

Don't let your familiarity with this verse dull its intended impact in your life. Today would be a great day to get a blessing for giving one.

The Lord told me to go, and he promised to send me far away to the Gentiles.

—Acts 22:21

As the apostle Paul recounted his life story and his glorious conversion, he related a conversation with the risen Lord. It was more like a friendly argument. Jesus instructed Paul to leave Jerusalem because the Jewish leaders wouldn't accept his message. And it could get dangerous.

Paul didn't understand. After all, with his impeccable Jewish credentials—even his involvement in the stoning of Stephen, the church's first martyr—how could they not listen to him?

But Jesus told him to leave and go to the Gentiles. Paul thought he had it all figured out. And it was a good plan. It just wasn't God's plan.

If you've got your life figured out, you may be shortchanging God's plan for you. Listen to Him.

I want you to open their eyes, so that they will turn from darkness to light and from the power of Satan to God. Then their sins will be forgiven, and by faith in me they will become part of God's holy people.

—*Acts 26:18*

W hy do we tell others about Jesus? Jesus Himself tells us, in these words spoken to Paul during his dramatic conversion on the road to Damascus.

He sends us to open the eyes of those who don't know Him. To invite them to see the reality of God in their very midst.

He sends us to turn people from darkness to light. Life without God is life without hope. But we can turn on the light of the truth by sharing the love of the Lord with others.

He sends us to lead people from the power of Satan to God.

He sends us to be His channel of forgiveness of sins. As He touches lives, the chains of sin are opened and fall to the ground.

He may be sending you this very day.

My kindness is all you need. My power is strongest when you are weak.

—2 Corinthians 12:9

Even when you seem plagued by a thorny sin that doesn't seem to let go.

Even when you are lost in confusion about a decision you must make.

Even when you are bound up by loneliness.

Even when you fail at a good intention.

Even when you struggle with another person.

Even when you feel you've made a selfish choice.

Even when you don't seem to be growing as fast as you'd like.

Even when doubts shake your confidence—even in the Lord of your life.

Even then, the Lord's kindness, or grace, is all you need.

Exchange your weakness—in whatever form you find it today—for His strength. He is sufficient.

I am Alpha and Omega, the one who is and was and is coming. I am God All-Powerful!

—*Revelation 1:8*

Jesus, the risen Lord and Savior, introduces Himself in the opening verses of the book of Revelation, written by the apostle John.

He is Alpha and Omega—the first and last letters of the Greek alphabet. The Beginning and the End. The eternal, the everlasting. The One who is over all from start to finish and beyond.

He is past, present, and future—the One who was and is and will be.

He is almighty—the all-powerful One.

He already knows your past. He is with you in your present struggles. He will always be with you in the future.

And still He loves you.

Knowing this, what is there in your life that you couldn't trust Him with?

[I am] the living one. I died, but now I am alive forevermore, and I have the keys to death and the world of the dead.

—*Revelation 1:18*

Assurance. Confidence. Certainty. That's what you can experience today because of what Jesus is saying about Himself.

He is God. He is alive. And He is powerful. With the keys to death and the world of the dead, Jesus possesses absolute control over life and death.

Your Savior appeared to John in glory and power decades after His death on the cross. He is still alive, still powerful, still reigning in heaven. And still concerned about His children, including you.

Jesus' absolute power and glory may seem fearful—as they did to John—but they are not intended to be. Rather than fear, Jesus intends to build confidence—in Him. He is alive; He is willing; He is able.

I know everything you have done, including your hard work and how you have endured. I know you won't put up with anyone who is evil. . . . You have endured and gone through hard times because of me, and you have not given up. But I do have something against you. . . . You don't have as much love as you used to.

—Revelation 2:2–4

Jesus the risen Lord sends a message to a church in John's day, the church at Ephesus. But it's a message that could be heard today in many churches by many individuals.

There is much to be praised. These believers work hard for God. They fight against evil. They have stood up against false teachers and patiently worked for good.

Yet, there's a problem. They had become second-generation believers. Their works were good but empty because they were not sourced in love. Love for Jesus. Love for others.

The motive was gone. The authenticity was absent. And that broke Jesus' heart. The main concern of the Lord is love.

Think about where you have fallen from, and then turn back and do as you did at first. If you don't turn back, I will come and take away your lampstand.

—Revelation 2:5

To the church at Ephesus, Jesus has sent a letter revealing His disappointment that their works were performed without love. They had lost their first love of Him. Now He tells them—and us—how to correct that situation.

Think about how it was, in the first blush of excited love for the Lord and for your fellow believers. Think of the energy you received from that love. And realize how far you've fallen from that lofty state. *Remember.*

Turn away from this empty existence. Change your mind about how things should be. *Repent.*

Come back to Him, and let Him rekindle your heart. Do again the things you used to do at first as a young follower basking in the glory of the new birth. *Return.*

DAY 336

If you have ears, listen to what the Spirit says to the churches. I will let everyone who wins the victory eat from the life-giving tree in God's wonderful garden.

—Revelation 2:7

Jesus makes a promise to you today. It's a promise of eternal life with Him. It's a promise of the paradise of God. It's a promise for the future, for eternity. And for right now.

But it's a promise for those who have ears to hear what the Spirit is saying. And it's a promise for those who win the victory.

Are you winning the victory? Sometimes in the midst of the frustrations and failures of life, the last thing that brings comfort is the far-flung promise of living in a heavenly paradise and eating the fruit of the tree of life.

But it's true, and He holds it out for us to reach for.

He's there already, waiting for you. And He's here, waiting to help you on your way there. Wanting to give you the grace and strength you need to overcome—to win the victory one more day.

DAY 337

Don't worry about what you will suffer. The devil will throw some of you into jail, and you will be tested and made to suffer for ten days. But if you are faithful until you die, I will reward you with a glorious life.

—Revelation 2:10

Jesus prepares the hearts of the believers at the church of Smyrna, warning them of sufferings ahead. But He encourages them not to fear. Even though they face a short period of tribulation, hope and purpose are in it all.

Keep at it, despite the challenges you face. Keep strong, keep standing, as you confront the tribulations of your life.

Be faithful, even though it may mean your death. Because you will receive a life that is far richer and deeper than life on earth could be.

Your life may appear relatively safe and simple compared to what the early Christians faced. Yet Satan is at work even today.

But Jesus holds out to you a glorious life for your faithfulness.

DECEMBER 2

If you have ears, listen to what the Spirit says to the churches. Whoever wins the victory will not be hurt by the second death.

—Revelation 2:11

The second death.

And you thought one death was bad enough. This one is far more serious, far worse. The second death is eternal death. Total separation from God. Eternity in hell. Because of sin, the destiny of every individual is the second death.

But thanks be to God, Jesus has provided the alternative. His sacrificial death on the cross on our behalf opens the door to heaven for everyone.

Once you've entered that door, once you've started on the path to overcoming failure and fear, you'll never be hurt by the second death.

That's Jesus' promise. Hear Him. Believe Him. Trust Him.

Following that path requires that we be victorious and overcome the difficulties life throws our way. And yet we *can* overcome in His strength and power, protected by His provision of love and grace.

I know that you live where Satan has his throne. But you have kept true to my name. Right there where Satan lives, my faithful witness Antipas was taken from you and put to death. Even then you did not give up your faith in me.

—Revelation 2:13

To the believers in the church at Pergamum— home of emperor worship and pagan idols— Jesus sends a word of comfort. You can receive it today, too.

The believers were faithful despite the challenges they lived with constantly. They held fast to Jesus, even when one of their number was put to death for his faith.

What would you do if a fellow believer was murdered simply for being a believer? Would you be tempted to hide your faith?

Not the believers at Pergamum. And Jesus honored their strength.

Yet, they were strong simply because He is. His strength strengthens us no matter where we live.

Turn back! If you don't, I will come quickly and fight against these people. And my words will cut like a sword.

—Revelation 2:16

The church at Pergamum was praised by Jesus, the risen Lord. Yet, He also had a few things against His followers there, namely, some of their beliefs. They had fallen prey to some unbiblical teachings of certain semi-Christian groups. And Jesus would have nothing to do with them.

Unless the Christians of Pergamum turned away from the false and harmful doctrines, He said He would come to fight against the falsehoods. And His words—the truth, the Word of God—would cut like a sword.

Jesus expects His children to know the truth—the truth that will set us free. And when we meander from it, willfully or ignorantly, He cares about our straying. In fact, He's willing to take action to prevent it.

Jesus is concerned about what you know and believe. How well do you know the truth? How well are you living it?

If you have ears, listen to what the Spirit says to the churches. To everyone who wins the victory, I will give some of the hidden food. I will also give each one a white stone with a new name written on it. No one will know that name except the one who is given the stone.

—Revelation 2:17

To the Christians at Pergamum, Jesus sends a word of challenge to overcome the false doctrine they had fallen into. And if they did, He would give them some of the "hidden food"—spiritual, heavenly food for believers. Perhaps it is a reference to Jesus Himself, the Bread of Life, who nourishes, fills, and satisfies.

What's more, Jesus would give each one a white stone with a new name written on it. Scholars have debated for centuries what Jesus means. Maybe He means a white stone with a new name written on it. Or maybe it signifies something much deeper. But Jesus promises to give a new name.

God names you. That means He accepts you. He parents you. He endows you with honor and authority.

I am the Son of God! My eyes are like flames of fire, and my feet are like bronze.

—Revelation 2:18

Jesus the man is never described in Scripture. We have no idea what He looked like.

But here, Jesus is described as the Son of God, with flaming eyes and feet like bronze, very reflective and bright.

He is fiery and shining. He possesses the flame of anger and righteous judgment against sin, the shiny reflection as though to reveal our sin as if we were gazing in a mirror.

Jesus is the glorious Son of God, the One who rules in authority and power. But He is also the One who desires righteousness and holiness in His children. The One who will do all within His power to create that righteousness and holiness in your heart.

I know everything about you, including your love, your faith, your service, and how you have endured. I know that you are doing more now than you have ever done before.

—Revelation 2:19

To the church at Thyatira, Jesus sends words of commendation. He honors their love, their faith, their service, and their endurance—certainly attributes that would be welcome in any believer's life.

In fact, He notes their later works are even greater than their earlier works. In other words, they're not cooling off. They're not burning out. They're growing.

You would think that's the way it's supposed to be, a natural result of knowing Jesus longer and following Him over the years. Yet when we look around us, we see that many believers grow tired and lazy in the faith. They lose the fire they had at first.

Learn from the example of the Thyatiran believers. It is possible to keep growing, to get better and better over the years—and then to hear the commendation of your Lord.

DAY 344

But until I come, you must hold firmly to the teaching you have.

—Revelation 2:25

To the faithful band of believers at the church of Thyatira, Jesus sends a word of encouragement. A word you can hear today, too.

Hold on to your faith. Hold firmly to the truths that give you hope and meaning. To your relationship with Jesus. To your commitment to grow step-by-step.

Hold firmly to the precious relationships you've built and sometimes must struggle with.

Hold firmly to the things in your life that bring joy and peace and pleasure.

Think of the things in your life you want to hold firmly to. Think of the things you may be loosening your grip on. Think of the things you're not holding on to that you'd like to get a grip on. He will come. Then you can let go, knowing it will all be right forever.

DECEMBER 9

I will give power over the nations to everyone who wins the victory and keeps on obeying me until the end.

—*Revelation 2:26*

Jesus makes another promise to those who win the victory over the struggles and strains of life. People who keep active in their faith, responsive to the Lord every day, even to the end, will be given something we may not be able to comprehend.

We will rule with Him. We will be shepherds to the nations. We will have authority with Him. That is, if we keep working with Him until the end. If we keep winning the victory.

Maybe power isn't much of an incentive for you. Maybe the promise of ruling with Christ over the nations really isn't that exciting to you.

The point to keep in mind today is, there is reward for being persistent in your faith. For keeping at it, even in the tough times. For not throwing in the towel when it gets lonely or weary or frightening.

There's promise, there's hope, there's confidence in the future, when you walk with Jesus.

Wake up! You have only a little strength left, and it is almost gone. So try to become stronger. I have found that you are not completely obeying God.

—Revelation 3:2

Is Jesus a perfectionist? Is He chastising the believers at Sardis for not completely obeying God?

Don't fall into that trap. The Bible is clear that none of us can ever live a perfect life in complete obedience. We are human. Faulty. Needy.

Even so, our desire should be to stay on a growth path. To keep working on becoming healthier and more whole. To acknowledge that only through the strength of Jesus can we do that. And to accept that there will be times when we fail.

But Jesus' words to the believers at Sardis can encourage us because we can identify with them and hear what He has to say. Keep strong. Stay spiritually alert and active.

Remember the teaching that you were given and that you heard. Hold firmly to it and turn from your sins. If you don't wake up, I will come when you least expect it, just as a thief does.

—Revelation 3:3

Jesus offers you three ways to think about your life and relationship with Him today. Three ways that offer balance and strength and growth.

First, remember how much you've learned about God and about yourself. Realize how much you were given in Him. And be thankful.

Second, compare what you know with what you're doing. Hold firmly to what you have, but let go of what is unhealthy and inhibiting.

Third, be ready for anything. Be strong in anticipating His return. Be growing when He finds you. Don't let Him surprise you by finding you unprepared to receive Him.

Keep these three bases of spiritual strength active in your life, and few things will be able to knock you over.

DAY 348

Everyone who wins the victory will wear white clothes. Their names will not be erased from the book of life, and I will tell my Father and his angels that they are my followers.

—Revelation 3:5

Jesus tells the believers at Sardis that if they win the victory, they will receive incomprehensible eternal blessings. They will be clothed in white, indicating eternal purity and righteousness. Their names will not be removed from the book of life, God's record of the redeemed. They will be named before the Father and His angels as Christ's own. They are eternally His. They cannot be replaced or rejected.

And if you win the victory, overcoming this life's obstacles and pains, you're part of that promise. When you triumph over your fears and faults and frustrations, when you keep moving forward with your Lord, you will receive these same incredible blessings from Him.

Look to Jesus for the encouragement. Look ahead to the culmination. And look within for the strength.

DECEMBER 13

I am the one who is holy and true, and I have the keys that belonged to David. When I open a door, no one can close it. And when I close a door, no one can open it.

—Revelation 3:7

Your Savior, by His own description, is holy. He is true. He has the authority of the universe—the keys of David—in His hands. What He does, no one can undo. What He doesn't do, no one can.

And what does all that mean to you? His Word is worth heeding. His life is worth emulating. His love is worth sharing. His comfort is worth claiming. His mercy is worth accepting. His will is worth obeying.

What else does it mean to you?

Think about these attributes of Jesus: His holiness and righteousness, His truth and honesty, His absolute authority and power. How do these attributes affect your life today? How do you respond to them?

I know everything you have done. And I have placed before you an open door that no one can close. You were not very strong, but you obeyed my message and did not deny that you are my followers.

—Revelation 3:8

An open door beckons. Jesus has put it there and opened it. And no one can close it.

Where does it lead? To an opportunity to serve? To a life of fulfillment with the Lord? To the kingdom of heaven itself?

If you could go anywhere, where would it be? If you could do anything, what would you do?

One of life's constant struggles is knowing where to go. Finding the best path. The most effective way. But the fact is, if you follow Jesus' word, live by the Spirit, stay open to His leading, and keep moving forward, the doors will open before you. And you can walk through them expectantly.

You obeyed my message and endured. So I will protect you from the time of testing that everyone in all the world must go through.

—Revelation 3:10

If you think things are bad today, just wait.

But better yet, continue to endure, or persevere. Then you won't have to be subjected to the testing that is to come.

The time will come, Jesus says, when the world will face a test to determine who each individual is serving in life: God or Satan. But there's an out: keeping Christ's instruction to persevere.

That's what the believers at the church of Philadelphia did. And why Jesus commended them. They faced a world opposed to their ways, both politically and religiously. They may have felt exposed to the world and its ways.

You may feel the same today. Keep Jesus' command to persevere. He will honor it.

I am coming soon. So hold firmly to what you have, and no one will take away the crown that you will be given as your reward.

—Revelation 3:11

When Jesus comes, He will come suddenly. Unexpectedly.

In light of that, Jesus says, hold firmly to what you have.

Keep walking with Him; keep striving for truth and mercy; keep pressing for the prize. You will be given a crown, a glorious token of the authority and position you will hold as a child of God in heaven. But it's a crown that can be taken away. Not that you wouldn't make it into heaven, but you could lose some of that eternal glory. Jesus will reward each of us on the basis of our perseverance in our walk of faith. Those who keep at it, holding firmly to their faith, surely deserve the greater rewards in heaven.

So think of this as an invitation from Jesus not to give up. Not to let go of what's important to you. Not to lose heart. Because He is coming soon.

Everyone who wins the victory will be made into a pillar in the temple of my God, and they will stay there forever. I will write on each of them the name of my God and the name of his city. It is the new Jerusalem that my God will send down from heaven. I will also write on them my own new name.

—Revelation 3:12

Jesus makes another promise to His children who win the victory over the troubles and tribulations of life: He will make them pillars in the temple of God.

His believers will hold a permanent place in heaven, in the bosom of the Father. We can stand tall and strong forever. No one can remove us, and *we* certainly won't want to leave.

Not only that, but Jesus promises to write the name of God, the name of the city of New Jerusalem, and His own new name on each of us.

Because we identify with Jesus Christ by becoming His followers, He identifies Himself with us. Totally. Without reservation. And forever.

I am the one called Amen! I am the faithful and true witness and the source of God's creation.

—*Revelation 3:14*

Jesus is the "Amen." *Amen* means "so be it." And these are the words of One who is in sovereign control of all human events. He has authority over everything that happens in your life.

He is the "faithful and true witness." Because His heart is always in the right place, and His words are always the truth, what He says is worth listening to. And heeding.

He is the "source of God's creation." He possesses full authority over everything that God created. He is the Ruler. He existed before time and creation, and He is the Sovereign of all. Everything is in His hands.

When Jesus says something to you, it has the full weight of eternity behind it. The full authority of the Father behind it. The full power of deity behind it. So receive it expectantly.

I know everything you have done, and you are not cold or hot. I wish you were either one or the other.

—*Revelation 3:15*

Lukewarm believers. That described the church at Laodicea. But you may confuse it with any other church today.

Cold believers are turned off to the heat of God's love. Perhaps God can reach into their hearts with the warmth of grace and acceptance, and light them up with the brightness of His love. But it's up to each believer to respond.

Hot believers' hearts burn with a godly passion. Their prayers are fervent, their service significant, their lives sail above the fray. Their spirits are kindled by the Holy Spirit.

Jesus would rather have a cold Christian than a lukewarm one who is lazy and weak, yet pretends to have it all together spiritually. Jesus can fan the embers in the heart. The Spirit can rekindle the flame if the believer will let Him.

You claim to be rich and successful and to have everything you need. But you don't know how bad off you are. You are pitiful, poor, blind, and naked.

—Revelation 3:17

In terms of money and possessions, they were wealthy. They needed nothing. But in terms of spiritual life and vitality, they were poor indeed.

That was Jesus' indictment of the lukewarm believers at the church of Laodicea. Their lives had been choked by material success; their spirits were drowned in the abundance of what they owned. And they didn't even know it.

Jesus looked at them and saw wretchedness. Misery. Poverty. Blindness. And the shame of nakedness. That was the spiritual truth, which was being denied by the believers.

To be blunt, they made Jesus sick (Rev. 3:16).

Complacency kills. Physical comforts strangle. Wealth withers spiritual vitality.

Take heed. Watch out for your heart and soul and spirit.

Buy your gold from me. It has been refined in a fire, and it will make you rich. Buy white clothes from me. Wear them and you can cover up your shameful nakedness. Buy medicine for your eyes, so that you will be able to see.

—Revelation 3:18

They were wealthy, but it was the world's tarnished wealth. So Jesus offered them true gold to make them truly rich.

They wore the finest in fashions, but their clothing left them naked and shamed. So Jesus offered them the white clothes of purity, righteousness, and holiness.

They thought they knew and understood the truth, but it was empty and ineffectual. So Jesus offered to anoint their eyes with the truth. Then they could see their need to turn their hearts back to Him.

You have the same Savior today. What do you think He yearns to give to you?

I correct and punish everyone I love. So make up
your minds to turn away from your sins.

—Revelation 3:19

Parenting keeps a child growing in the right direction. Free of unnecessary restrictions, yet with
a guiding hand that keeps the child from wandering too far off the general path of healthiness.

Sometimes a child's errors bring their own discipline. Other times the parent must carefully explain the wrong and impose the discipline.

This is what Jesus does to His children because
He loves us.

As a father or mother loves the children and
would do anything for them, so Jesus desires to
rebuke and chasten those who have wandered
from the way of health and godliness.

Therefore, He says, make up your mind to
turn away from sins. Before He has to do something drastic to get your attention, be proactive.
Open yourself to His truth.

Listen! I am standing and knocking at your door. If you hear my voice and open the door, I will come in and we will eat together.

—Revelation 3:20

Jesus, your Savior, stands at the door, knocking. He wants you to hear His greeting, to open the door, to invite Him in.

The door represents His entryway into your everyday life. And when you open it, He promises to come in and share a meal with you. To talk over what's going on. To laugh, to share concerns, to enjoy each other's company.

That's friendship—a rich relationship of joy and camaraderie and concern.

And Jesus offers it to His children. In this verse, He offers it to the believers at Laodicea— the lukewarm believers Jesus threatened to spit out of His mouth in disgust for their laziness and complacency.

If He is willing to make this invitation to them, what must He feel about you?

Do you hear His voice? Will you open the door?

DAY 360

Everyone who wins the victory will sit with me on my throne, just as I won the victory and sat with my Father on his throne.

—Revelation 3:21

Jesus faced the absolute epitome of tribulation: cruel mockery, vicious abuse, a violent and barbaric death. And yet He speaks to us today triumphant, victorious. Because He rose again. He ascended into heaven. And He sat with His Father to rule from the throne of the universe. Now *that*'s a victory.

And He extends an invitation to His children to join Him on that same throne. He encourages us to face the problems of life, the tests and trials and tribulations. And with His strength, to stand empowered in the face of the problems. To win over them.

When we do, we will be granted the authority to sit with Him in heaven. To share in His reign of the universe.

What does that mean exactly? We can't know until then. But you *will* know if you follow His example and draw on His strength—no matter what tribulations you face.

DECEMBER 25

When I come, it will surprise you like a thief! But God will bless you, if you are awake and ready. Then you won't have to walk around naked and be ashamed.

—Revelation 16:15

Thieves come in the dead of the dark night to take what is precious away for themselves. You don't plan on having them come to visit you. They come secretly, unexpectedly.

Jesus says He will return to earth just like a thief. But He urges His children to watch for Him. Be ready for Him. Don't even undress for bed—but be clothed and ready to respond when He comes.

The alternative is to fall asleep in the faith so that when the "thief" comes, we would be caught off guard, unprepared, unclothed, and therefore ashamed.

That's certainly not His desire for us. He wants to bless us. So He wants us to be ready for Him.

Clothe yourself with His robes of righteousness, the ones He gave you when He first saved you.

I am coming soon! God will bless everyone who pays attention to what this book tells about the future.

—Revelation 22:7

Jesus repeats the same message through the book of Revelation: "I am coming soon!" Have you gotten the message yet?

This time, He backs it with yet another promise of blessing for those who keep the words of the prophecy that John has recorded in this book.

The message is clear: God is in control of the future. There will come a time when history reaches a climax, Christ returns, and eternal life is inaugurated. And because that time is coming, His children are urged to be ready for it.

You can gain encouragement from the book of Revelation as it reveals kingly power and heavenly worship. Read it. Heed it. And you will be blessed. That's Jesus' promise to you.

I am coming soon! And when I come, I will reward everyone for what they have done.

—Revelation 22:12

When Jesus returns to earth, He will bring a reward. It is for His children only. And it is given strictly according to our works.

"But wait!" you may protest. "What do works have to do with eternity? I thought salvation was a gift of God, and nothing I do or don't do can cause it or keep it from me."

And you would be correct. Salvation is assured to those who trust Christ. No works are necessary for eternal life with Him in heaven. But Jesus makes it clear (as does Paul in 2 Cor. 5:10) that our works will have an impact on our experience of eternity in heaven.

No matter what the reward may be, you will enjoy eternity as His child. But your experience can be eternally richer, more fulfilling, more enjoyable, because of your giving and serving and loving here on earth.

DAY 364

I am Alpha and Omega, the first and the last, the beginning and the end.

—Revelation 22:13

Jesus is eternal. He existed before time and creation. In fact, He was the agent of creation. He reigns now in heaven, actively interceding for His children as Advocate. He will return to earth in the future and usher in eternity. And there He will rule in might and majesty forever.

He is before all and after all. He is the start and the finish. He is all and in all. And everything in between.

Jesus' descriptions in the book of Revelation speak of His absolute power and authority. His fierce resolve to carry out the Father's plan. His unyielding desire to be righteousness and justice personified.

But in the immensity and gravity of these descriptions, don't lose sight of His love and concern right now for you. You, His precious child. That love undergirds everything He does or says.

I am Jesus! And I am the one who sent my angel to tell all of you these things for the churches. I am David's Great Descendant, and I am also the bright morning star.

—Revelation 22:16

Jesus has the authority to reveal these truths, for He is the King of the universe.

He is David's "Great Descendant." He is of the lineage of the king of Israel, and He assumes that role forever. He is the Son of God and the Son of man.

So He alone is qualified to atone for humanity's sins. He alone is equipped to rule the universe. And He alone is able to understand each of us from the inside out because He was one of us.

He is the "bright morning star." His coming shines in the night, leading the way to a new daybreak that will change the face of the earth. And transform each of our lives. In His radiant holiness and power, He will rule forever.

In the same way, He can rule today in your life if you will listen to Him.

I am coming soon!
—Revelation 22:20

When Jesus came to earth as a human baby, things changed. He sent a tiny nation into an uproar. People swarmed about Him, seeking His touch, giving their lives to Him.

He drove an entrenched religious leadership over the edge. Stung by His painfully honest rebukes, they battled Him to the death: His own.

But it was all in the plan of the Father. For His death opened the door for you to join Him, to be with Him forever.

Today, it's still happening. All around the world. And in your own heart.

Jesus came to the world to bring salvation to those who would hear and answer His call. He will come again to bring the final deliverance.

His final words recorded in Scripture give us hope to keep on keeping on until the final day arrives. With John the apostle we agree: "So, Lord Jesus, please come soon!" (Rev. 22:20).

SUBJECT INDEX

Abandonment, 228
Abba, 36
Abundance, 114
Abuse, 30, 156
Acceptance, 95, 155, 169, 175, 220, 262, 284, 316, 323, 341
Accepting, 149
Adoration, 312
Alienation, 159
Alive, 333
Allegiance, 190
Anger, 11, 21, 181, 199, 297, 298
Answers, 140, 210
Apathy, 102
Asking, 134
Asking God, 51, 52
Attitudes, 49
Authenticity, 56, 132
Authority, 63, 142, 178, 194, 227, 230, 234, 256, 345, 354
Awesome, 364

Balance, 193
Barrenness, 104
Beginnings, 244
Behavior, 9
Belief, 260, 281
Beliefs, 55

Betrayal, 152, 284, 313
Bitterness, 38, 40, 167
Blessings, 116, 328, 362
Body of Christ, 327
Burdens, 96, 97

Camaraderie, 359
Celebration, 189, 237
Change, 18, 236
Chaos, 230, 314
Chastisement, 79
Childlikeness, 153, 154, 158, 182
Children, 155, 156, 161, 169, 285
Choices, 63
Church, 141
Circumstances, 128, 173, 232, 255
Cleansing, 39, 58, 200, 244, 259, 271, 282, 289
Close-mindedness, 318
Coldness, 17, 187
Comfort, 8, 97, 197
Commands, 282
Commitment, 242, 363
Communication, 179, 270, 296
Communion, 159, 219, 220
Companionship, 6, 222
Compassion, 13, 29, 73, 125, 135, 158, 166, 258, 259

Complacency, 356
Confession, 38
Confidence, 4, 51, 57, 79, 82, 83, 94, 302, 333
Conflict, 13
Confrontation, 9, 162, 201
Confusion, 1, 113, 247, 350, 362
Consequences, 64, 262, 279
Control, 230, 333
Conversation, 105, 106
Convictions, 181
Costliness, 312
Courage, 255
Covenant, 220
Creativity, 252

Darkness, 330
Death, 107, 149, 260, 338
Deception, 204
Decisions, 253, 350
Deity, 318
Delight, 122
Deliverance, 366
Denial, 356
Denying Jesus, 313, 316
Dependence on God, 7
Desires, 23
Despair, 8
Differences, 291
Difficulties, 86
Direction, 253, 315

Directness, 273, 296
Disappointment, 224
Discernment, 42, 55, 76, 91, 132, 133, 180, 204
Disciples, 231
Discipleship, 80
Discipline, 358
Dissatisfaction, 4
Distance, 267
Distractions, 111, 278
Divisions, 86, 101, 242
Doubt, 45, 52, 72, 124, 127, 128, 180, 183, 234, 281
Dullness, 17, 19

Embarrassment, 283
Emotions, 21
Empowerment, 299, 360
Emptiness, 357
Encouragement, 7, 106, 258, 280, 348, 362
Endurance, 206
Enemies, 28, 29
Equality, 196
Eternal life, 191
Eternity, 83, 198, 309, 364
Evil, 117, 256, 272, 339
Exclusion, 286
Excuses, 61
Expectancy, 310
Eyes, 42

Failure, 243, 283

Faith, 56, 59, 62, 70, 72, 79, 124, 150, 151, 183, 184, 240, 255, 259, 298, 299

Faithfulness, 212, 213, 337, 339

Faithlessness, 107

False doctrines, 340

Familiarity, 19

Family, 108

Fantasies, 131

Father, 197

Fear, 62, 65, 81, 126, 128, 148, 215, 223, 228, 254, 257, 260, 265, 307, 324, 337

Fellowship, 163, 287, 359

Femininity, 291

Flesh, 225

Following Jesus, 6, 60, 61, 66, 85, 88, 92, 144, 174, 286

Forgiveness, 11, 24, 31, 38, 40, 64, 65, 103, 156, 165, 166, 167, 244, 269, 300, 301, 330

Forthrightness, 25

Foundations, 57

Fraud, 297

Freedom, 44, 68, 167, 257, 258, 325

Friends, 28, 29, 196

Friendship, 313

Fruitfulness, 104, 112, 188

Frustration, 150, 275

Fulfillment, 97, 118, 137, 226

Fullness, 121

Future, 48, 308

Generosity, 165

Genuineness, 268

Gifts, 214, 215

Giving, 27, 32, 75, 304, 328

Glory, 209, 227, 280, 332

God's care, 84

God's love, 45

God's people, 188

God's plan, 305, 310, 329

God's presence, 309

God's timing, 321

God's will, 3, 211, 223, 298, 315, 317

God's Word, 19

Golden rule, 53

Goodness, 170

Grace, 69, 99, 319, 331, 346

Greatness, 153

Grief, 125

Growth, 89, 104, 109, 110, 112, 118, 251, 276, 310, 331, 343

Grudges, 166, 300

Guidance, 194, 204

Hardened hearts, 100, 103, 109, 199

Hardships, 15, 54

Healing, 59, 67, 72, 236, 240, 241

Heart, 105, 106, 130, 131, 248, 304
Heaven, 158, 336
Hiding, 249
Hindrances, 110, 171, 172, 203, 274, 292, 293
Holding on, 344, 352
Holiness, 200, 349, 364
Holy Spirit, 320, 322
Honesty, 21, 133, 134, 182, 272, 349
Hope, 191, 221, 366
Hopelessness, 206
Humanity, 233, 346
Humiliation, 295
Humility, 9, 26, 154, 177, 188, 195, 198, 218
Hunger, 135, 136, 264
Hurts, 15, 40
Hypocrisy, 201

Identification, 323, 353
Impatience, 276
Impermanence, 203
Inadequacy, 82, 136
Inclusiveness, 187, 297, 319
Individuality, 168
Indwelling, 116
Influence, 119
Inheritance, 216
Inner child, 285
Internal life, 200, 201, 271

Intimacy, 35, 95, 197, 317
Invitation, 164, 189, 207, 213, 216, 359
Involvement, 102

Jesus' identity, 140
Jesus' presence, 116, 164, 232, 237
Jesus' return, 209
Journey, 253
Judging, 49, 50, 56, 133
Judgment, 117, 189, 342
Judgmentalism, 172
Justice, 186

Kingdom, 74, 120, 121, 122, 175, 190

Laziness, 215, 225, 343, 355
Leading, 324
Learning, 139, 196, 245
Legalism, 20, 170
Lethargy, 10
Letting go, 46
Life, 60, 84, 89, 132, 145
Light, 249
Listening, 210, 245, 250, 270
Loneliness, 68
Loss, 221, 314
Lostness, 159
Love, 28, 30, 31, 32, 33, 53, 78, 90, 161, 179, 193, 195, 207, 268, 303, 334, 358

Loving God, 192
Lukewarmness, 355
Lust, 23

Malaise, 73
Marriage, 168
Masculinity, 291
Materialism, 41, 171
Maturity, 154, 343
Meaning, 130, 266
Mercy, 11, 67, 92, 98, 99
Message, 306
Mind, 192
Ministering, 42
Ministry, 263
Miracles, 71, 261
Mockery, 295
Money, 43
Morality, 23
Motivation, 147
Motives, 3, 32, 334
Mystery, 246

Names, 341
Neediness, 27, 51, 135, 148, 217
Needs, 238
New, 123
New life, 5, 69

Obedience, 1, 5, 14, 27, 57, 63, 66, 93, 100, 127, 144, 180, 248, 256, 270, 282, 292, 325
Obsessions, 44

Offenses, 165
Openness, 91, 94, 95, 115, 139, 185, 187, 203, 241, 248, 274, 277, 279, 318, 326
Opportunities, 76, 218, 273, 307, 350
Opposition, 78, 205
Ostracism, 70
Overcoming, 336, 341, 348, 353
Overwhelmed, 264

Pain, 84, 87, 228, 295
Paranoia, 311
Parents, 269
Passion, 69, 98
Path, 54
Peace, 76, 254, 265
Peacemaking, 13
Perfection, 171
Perfectionism, 346
Permanence, 353
Persecution, 14, 15, 80, 81, 323
Perseverance, 351
Persistence, 179, 273, 345
Physical life, 37, 47
Poor, 218
Possessions, 293
Poverty, 304
Power, 62, 75, 126, 138, 148, 150, 177, 208, 234, 236, 242, 243, 254, 257, 261, 281, 317, 320, 322, 332, 349

Powerlessness, 124, 184
Praise, 182
Prayer, 35, 36, 37, 58, 59, 163,
    164, 184, 235, 299, 300
Presence, 320
Preservation, 290
Pride, 20, 34, 137, 195
Priorities, 47, 61, 87, 88, 98, 267,
    278, 305, 316, 344
Problems, 360
Process, 145
Progress, 303
Promise, 33, 82, 152, 216, 336,
    338, 348
Promises, 114, 226
Protection, 90, 296, 338
Purification, 289
Purity, 12, 272
Purpose, 89, 235, 239
Pursuing God, 12

Radical living, 78
Rationalizing, 329
Reaching out, 16, 31, 50, 70, 74,
    155, 160, 199, 207, 217, 231,
    287, 330
Readiness, 212, 213, 366
Reality, 146
Receiving, 52, 285, 288, 328, 354
Reconciliation, 22, 49, 101, 162
Reigning, 194, 342

Rejection, 202
Rejoicing, 160, 229
Rekindling, 335
Relationships, 22, 53, 86, 87, 90,
    108, 162, 168, 193, 224, 344
Release, 243
Remembering, 136, 219, 221,
    335, 347
Repentance, 5, 335, 340, 347
Resources, 264
Responding, 18, 66, 93, 109, 110,
    112, 141, 185, 261, 308
Response, 6, 324
Responsibilities, 34, 190, 251,
    263, 269
Responsibility, 122, 240
Responsiveness, 233, 262
Rest, 96, 239, 263
Restoration, 22
Restrictions, 326
Results, 251
Resurrection, 191, 229, 315, 321
Revenge, 26, 301
Reward, 30, 33, 41, 91, 147, 206,
    212, 214, 288, 345, 352, 363
Riches, 294
Righteousness, 14, 20, 181, 342,
    361
Rights, 174, 301
Rigidity, 99, 129, 138, 238, 241,
    266, 268, 303, 325

Risk, 1, 58, 125, 127, 151, 176, 312
Routines, 55
Rulership, 365
Rules, 129, 238

Sacrifice, 60, 73, 88, 120, 174, 219, 223, 288
Salvation, 173
Satisfaction, 43
Scripture, 123
Secrets, 35, 113
Security, 83, 294
Self-centeredness, 105
Self-deception, 292
Self-defeat, 65
Self-denial, 144
Self-effort, 170
Self-examination, 50, 85
Self-preparation, 208, 211, 283, 305, 308, 347, 361
Self-protection, 67, 284
Self-sacrifice, 293
Selfishness, 10, 120
Servanthood, 177, 178, 198
Service, 74, 75, 80, 92, 147
Serving God, 214
Shame, 237, 279
Sharing, 306
Shining, 246, 249
Shut down, 274

Sidetracked, 271
Signs, 275
Sin, 24, 64
Sincerity, 77
Single-mindedness, 12
Slowness, 277
Smallness, 118
Solitude, 34, 102, 235
Sorrow, 8, 152, 222
Soul, 192
Speaking, 307
Spiritual blindness, 137, 186, 276
Spiritual deadness, 266
Spiritual highs, 280
Spiritual hunger, 2, 10, 68, 250
Spiritual life, 142, 278
Spiritual light, 17
Spiritual thirst, 16
Stagnation, 85
Stewardship, 43
Storms, 265
Strangers, 217
Strength, 26, 37, 141, 146, 157, 205, 302, 327, 339
Struggles, 46, 101, 126, 183
Stubbornness, 103, 114, 130, 186, 187
Study, 247
Stumbling, 121, 157
Success, 357
Suffering, 176, 289, 337

Supernatural, 138
Support, 108, 222, 224, 314, 327
Surprises, 71, 211, 361
Surrender, 145

Taking a stand, 81
Taking time, 163
Teaching, 231
Temptation, 2, 3, 4, 24, 39, 41,
    111, 143, 157
Tenacity, 134
Tenderness, 161
Testing, 140
Thirst, 290
Thoughtfulness, 143
Thoughts, 131
Time, 239
Today, 48
Tolerance, 286
Traditions, 129, 267
Transformation, 119, 153, 365
Trials, 351
Tribulation, 205, 360
Troubles, 117
Trust, 71, 175, 202, 208, 210, 226,
    232, 233, 294, 311, 332, 365
Trusting God, 2
Trustworthiness, 25
Truth, 25, 94, 115, 143, 227,
    246, 250, 252, 302, 340, 354

Unbelief, 151, 185, 275, 309
Understanding, 93, 113, 115, 123,
    139, 149, 247, 252, 277, 329
Unfairness, 39
Unhealthiness, 178
Uselessness, 16

Value, 45
Values, 146

Waiting, 245, 321
Walking with Jesus, 54
Wandering, 18, 160, 352
Warmth, 290, 355
Watchfulness, 142, 311
Weakness, 7, 331
Wealth, 172, 173, 356, 357
Weariness, 96
Wholeness, 100
Willfulness, 358
Willingness, 107, 176, 202, 225
Wisdom, 77
Witnessing, 322
Wonder, 169
Work, 47
Works, 334, 363
World, 77, 111, 119, 306, 319,
    326, 351
Worries, 44, 46, 48
Worship, 36, 209, 229